ART BOOKS

FROM CRESCENT MOON PUBLISHING

Leonardo da Vinci
by James Pearson

Early Netherlandish Painting
by Rosalind Mutter

Piero della Francesca
by Naomi Haskell

Giovanni Bellini
by Julia Davis

Eric Gill: Nuptials of God
by Anthony Hoyland

Minimal Art and Artists In the 1960s and After
by Laura Garrard

Postwar Art
by George Knighton

Vincent van Gogh: Visionary Landscapes
by Stuart Morris

Max Beckmann
by Stuart Morris

Egon Schiele: Sex and Death in Purple Stockings
by D. Simon Eade

Mark Rothko: The Art of Transcendence
by Julia Davis

Jasper Johns
by L.M. Poole

Brice Marden
by Laura Garrard

Frank Stella: American Abstract Artist
by James Pearson

BERNARDINO LUINI

BERNARDINO LUINI

BY JAMES MASON

CRESCENT MOON

First published 1908. This edition © 2020.

Set in Book Antiqua 10 on 14pt.
Designed by Radiance Graphics.

Thanks to the authors and publishers quoted.

British Library Cataloguing in Publication data

ISBN-13 9781861716484 (Pbk)
ISBN-13 9781861717726 (Pbk)
ISBN-13 9781861717153 (Hbk)

CRESCENT MOON PUBLISHING
P.O. Box 1312, Maidstone, Kent, ME14 5XU
Great Britain, www.crmoon.com

CONTENTS

NOTE ON THE TEXT

The text is from *Bernardo Luini* by James Mason, and published by Frederick A. Stokes Company, New York, 1908.

The illustrations in the original text are included in the illustrations section, along with many other works.

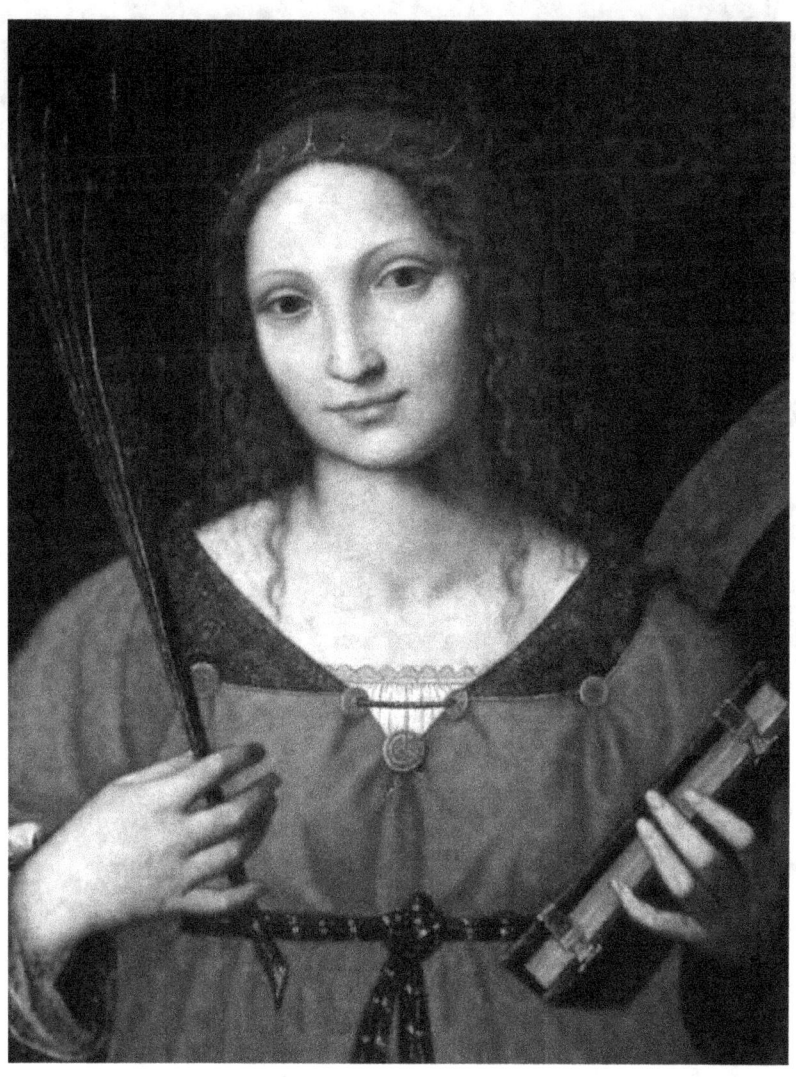

Bernardino Luini, St Catherine, Baku

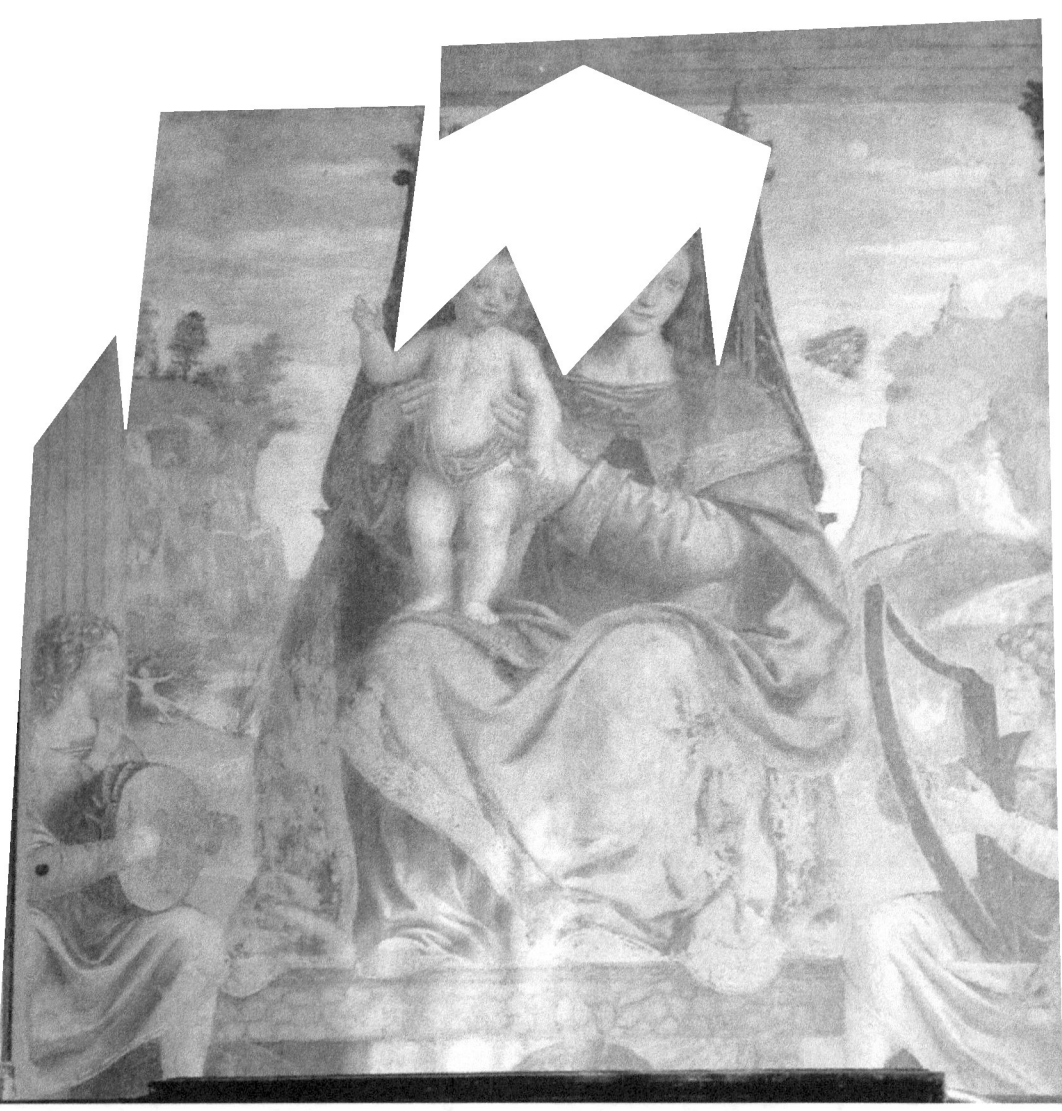

Bernardino Luini, Madonna Buonanotte, Milan

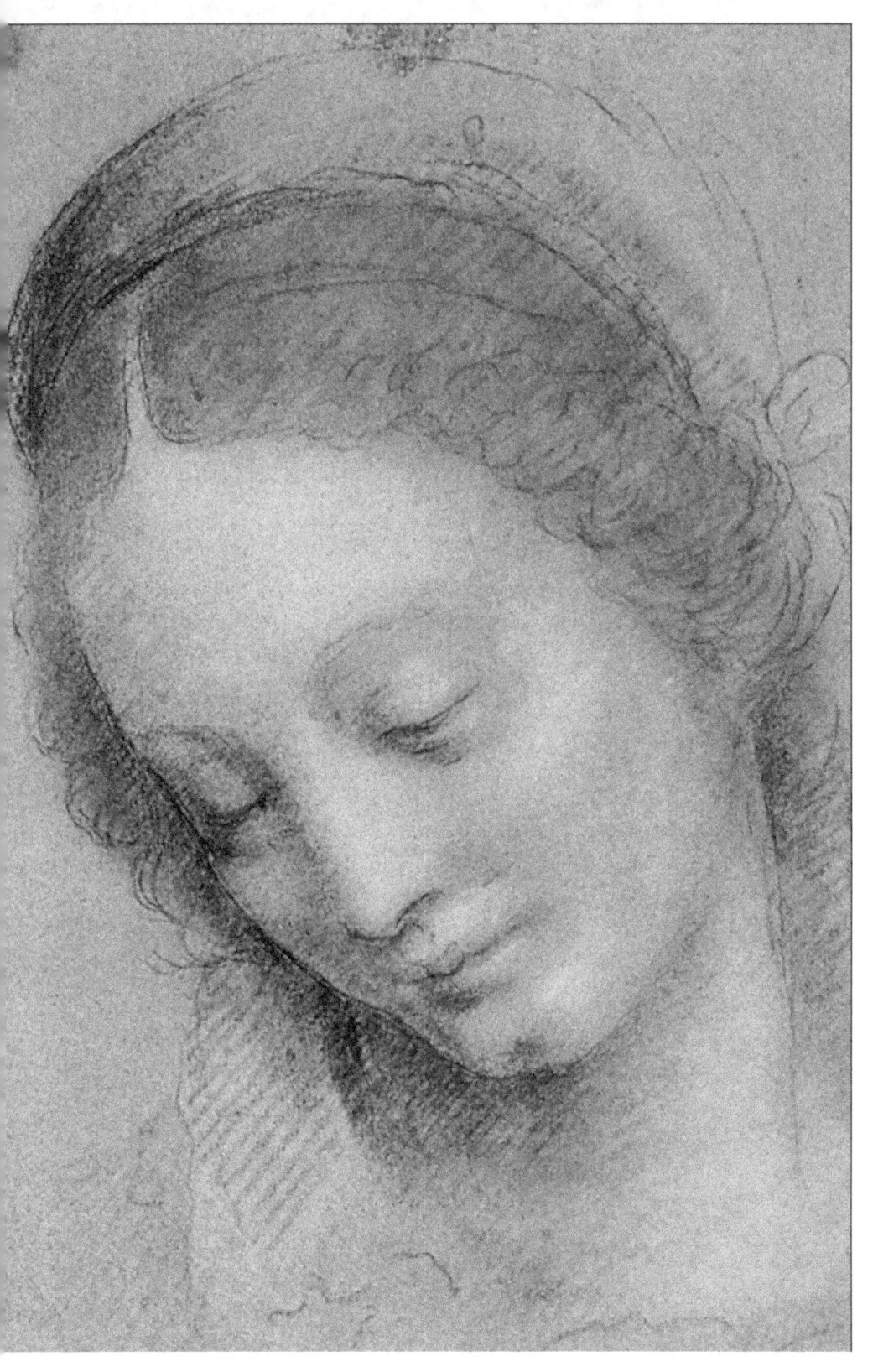

Bernardino Luini, Study For Head of a Woman

I

A RETROSPECT

In the beginning of the long and fascinating history of Italian Art we see that the spirit of the Renaissance first fluttered over the minds of men much as the spirit of life is said have moved over the face of the waters before the first chapter of creation's marvellous story was written. Beginnings were small, progress was slow, and the lives of the great artists moved very unevenly to their appointed end.

There were some who rose to fame and fortune during their life, and then died so completely that no biography can hope to rouse any interest in their work among succeeding generations.

There were others who worked in silence and without *réclame* of any sort, content with the respect and esteem of those with whom they came into immediate contact, indifferent to the plaudits of the crowd or the noisy praises of those who are not qualified to judge. True servants of the western world's religion, they translated work into terms of moral life, and moral life into terms of work. Merit like truth will out, and when time has sifted good work from bad and spurious reputations from genuine ones, many men who fluttered the dovecotes of their own generation disappear from sight altogether; some others who wrought unseen, never striving to gain the popular ear or eye, rise on a sudden to heights that might have made them giddy had they lived to be conscious of their own elevation. They were lowly, but their fame inherits the earth.

Bernardino Luini, the subject of this little study, calls us away from the great art centres – from Venice and Florence and Rome; his record was made and is to be found to-day amid the plains of Lombardy. Milan is not always regarded as one of the great art centres of Italy in spite of the Brera, the Ambrosiana, and the Poldi Pezzoli Palace collections, but no lover of pictures ever went for the first time to the galleries of Milan in a reverent spirit and with a patient eye without feeling that he had discovered a painter of genius. He may not even have heard his name before, but he will come away quite determined to learn all he may about the man who painted the wonderful frescoes that seem destined to retain their spiritual beauty till the last faint trace of the design passes beyond the reach of the eye, the man who painted the panel picture of the "Virgin of the Rose Trees," reproduced with other of his master-works in these pages.

To go to the Brera is to feel something akin to hunger for the history of Bernardino Luini or Luino or Luvino as he is called by the few who have found occasion to mention him, although perhaps Luini is the generally accepted and best known spelling of the name. Unfortunately the hungry feeling cannot be fully satisfied. Catalogues or guide books date the year of Luini's birth at or about 1470, and tell us that he died in 1533, and as this is a period that Giorgio Vasari covers, we turn eagerly to the well-remembered volumes of the old gossip hoping to find some stories of the Lombard painter's life and work. We are eager to know what manner of man Luini was, what forces influenced him, how he appeared to his contemporaries, whether he had a fair measure of the large success that attended the leading artists of his day. Were his patrons great men who rewarded him as he deserved – how did he fare when the evening came wherein no man may work? Surely there is ample scope for the score of quaint comments and amusing if unreliable anecdotes with which Vasari livens his pages. We are confident that there will be much to reward the search, because Bernardino Luini and Giorgio Vasari were contemporaries after a fashion. Vasari would have been twenty-one years old when Luini died, the writer of the "Lives" would have seen frescoes and panel pictures in all the glory of their first creation. He could not have failed to be impressed by the extraordinary beauty of the artist's conceptions, the skill of his treatment of single figures, the wealth of the curious and elusive charm that we call atmosphere – a charm to which all the world's masterpieces are indebted in varying degrees – the all-pervading sense of a delightful and refined personality, leaves us eager for the facts that must have been well within the grasp of the painter's contemporaries.

Alas for these expectations! Vasari dismisses Bernardino del Lupino, as he calls him, in six or eight sentences, and what he says has no biographical value at all. The reference reads suspiciously like what is known in the world of journalism as padding. Indeed, as Vasari was a fair judge, and Bernardino Luini was not one of those Venetians whom Vasari held more or less in contempt, there seems to be some reason for the silence. Perhaps it was an intimate and personal one, some unrecorded bitterness between the painter and one of Vasari's friends, or between Vasari himself and Luini or one of his brothers or children. Whatever the cause there is no mistake about the result. We grumble at Vasari, we ridicule his inaccuracies, we regret his limitations, we scoff at his prejudices, but when he withholds the light of his investigation from contemporary painters who did not enjoy the favour of popes and emperors, we wander in a desert land without a guide, and search with little or no success for the details that would serve to set the painter before us.

Many men have taken up the work of investigation, for Luini grows steadily in favour and esteem, but what Vasari might have done in a week nobody has achieved in a decade.

A few unimportant church documents relating to commissions

given to the painter are still extant. He wrote a few words on his frescoes; here and there a stray reference appears in the works of Italian writers of the sixteenth and seventeenth centuries, but our knowledge when it has been sifted and arranged is remarkably small and deplorably incomplete. Dr. J. C. Williamson, a painstaking critic and a competent scholar, has written an interesting volume dealing with the painter, and in the making of it he has consulted nearly fifty authorities – Italian, French, English, and German – only to find it is impossible to gather a short chapter of reliable and consecutive biography from them all. Our only hope lies in the discovery of some rich store of information in the public or private libraries of Milan among the manuscripts that are the delight of the scholars. Countless documents lie unread, many famous libraries are uncatalogued, the archives of several noble Italian houses that played an important part in fifteenth and sixteenth century Italy have still to be given to the world. It is not unreasonable to suppose that records of Luini's life exist, and in these days when scholarship is ever extending its boundaries there is hope that some scholar will lay the ever growing circle of the painter's admirers under lasting obligations. Until that time comes we must be content to know the man through the work that he has left behind him, through the medium of fading frescoes, stray altarpieces, and a few panel pictures. Happily they have a definite and pleasant story to tell.

We must go to Milan for Luini just as we must go to Rome for Raphael and to Madrid for Velazquez and Titian and to Venice for Jacopo Robusti whom men still call the Little Dyer (Tintoretto). In London we have one painting on wood, "Christ and the Pharisees," brought from the Borghese Palace in Rome. The head of Christ is strangely feminine, the four Pharisees round him are finely painted, and the picture has probably been attributed to Leonardo da Vinci at some period of its career. There are three frescoes in South Kensington and a few panel pictures in private collections. The Louvre is more fortunate than our National Gallery, it has several frescoes and two or three panels. In

Switzerland, in the Church of St. Mary and the Angels in Lugano, is a wonderful screen picture of the "Passion of Christ" with some hundreds of figures in it, and the rest of Luini's work seems to be in Italy. The greater part is to be found in Milan, some important frescoes having been brought to the Brera from the house of the Pelucca family in Monza, while there are some important works in Florence in the Pitti and Uffizi Galleries. In the Church of St. Peter at Luino on the shores of Lake Maggiore, the little town where Benardino was born and from which he took his name, there are some frescoes but they are in a very faded condition. The people of the lake side town have much to say about the master who has made Luino a place of pilgrimage but their stories are quite unreliable.

It might be held, seeing that the artist's work is scanty, and often in the last stages of decay, while his life story has faded quite from the recovered records of his contemporaries, that Luini is hardly fit subject for discussion here. In a series of little books that seeks to introduce great artists to new friends through the medium of reproductions that show the work as it is, and a brief concise description that aims at helping those who are interested to study the master for themselves, there is a temptation to deal only with popular men. These give no trouble to their biographer or his readers, but after all it is not the number of pictures that an artist paints or the wealth of detail that his admirers have collected that establishes his claim to be placed among the immortals. His claim rests upon the quality of the work done, its relation to the times in which it was painted, the mood or spirit it reveals, the light it throws upon the mind that conceived and the hand that executed it.

We know enough and to spare of the more flamboyant personalities of the Venetian and Florentine schools. Long periods of study will not exhaust all there is to learn about men like Titian, Michelangelo, Raphael of Urbino, and the rest, but Luini, though he left no written record, will not be denied. We dare not pass him by, seeing that we may introduce him to some admirers who will, in days to come, seek and find what remains beyond our reach at present. His appeal is so irresistible, the beauty of his work is so rare and so enduring that we must endeavour to the best of our ability, however small it be, to declare his praise, to stimulate inquiry, enlarge his circle, and give him the place that belongs to him of right. There are painters in plenty whose work is admired and praised, whose claims we acknowledge instantly while admitting to ourselves that we should not care to live with their pictures hanging on round us. The qualities of cleverness and brilliance pall after a little time, the mere conquest of technical difficulties of the kind that have been self-inflicted rouses admiration for a while and then leaves us cold. But the man who is the happy possessor of a fresco or a panel picture by Luini is to be envied. Even he who lives in the neighbourhood of some gallery or church and only sees the rare master's works where, "blackening in the daily candle smoke, they moulder on the damp wall's travertine," will never tire of Luini's company. He will always find inspiration, encouragement, or consolation in the reflection of the serene and beautiful outlook upon life that gave the work so much of its enduring merit. Luini, whatever manner of man he may have been, was so clearly enamoured of beauty, so clearly intolerant of what is ugly and unrefined, that he shrank from all that was coarse and revolting either in the life around him or in certain aspects of the Bible stories that gave him subjects for his brush. Beauty and simplicity were the objects of his unceasing search, his most exquisite expression.

Like all other great painters he had his marked periods of development, his best work was done in the last years of his life, but there is nothing mean or trivial in any picture that he painted and this is the more to his credit because we know from the documents existing to-day that he lived in the world and not in the cloister. We admire the perennial serenity of Beato Angelico, we rejoice with him in his exquisite religious visions. The peaceful quality of his painting and the happy certainty of his faith move us to the deepest admiration, but we may not forget that Angelico lived from the time when he was little more than a boy to the years when he was an old man in the untroubled atmosphere of the monastery of San Marco in Florence, that whether he was at home in that most favoured city or working in the Vatican at Rome, he had no worldly troubles. Honour, peace, and a mind at peace with the world were with him always.

Bernardino Luini on the other hand travelled from one town in Italy to another, employed by religious houses from time to time, but always as an artist who could be relied upon to do good work cheaply. He could not have been rich, he could hardly have been famous, it is even reasonable to suppose that his circumstances were straitened, and on this account the unbroken serenity of his work and his faithful devotion to beauty are the more worthy of our praise. What was beautiful in his life and work came from within, not from without, and perhaps because he was a stranger to the cloistered seclusion that made Fra Angelico's life so pleasantly uneventful his work shows certain elements of strength that are lacking from the frescoes that adorn the walls of San Marco to this day. To his contemporaries he was no more than a little planet wandering at will round those fixed stars of the first magnitude that lighted all the world of art. Now some of those great stars have lost their light and the little planet shines as clear as Hesperus.

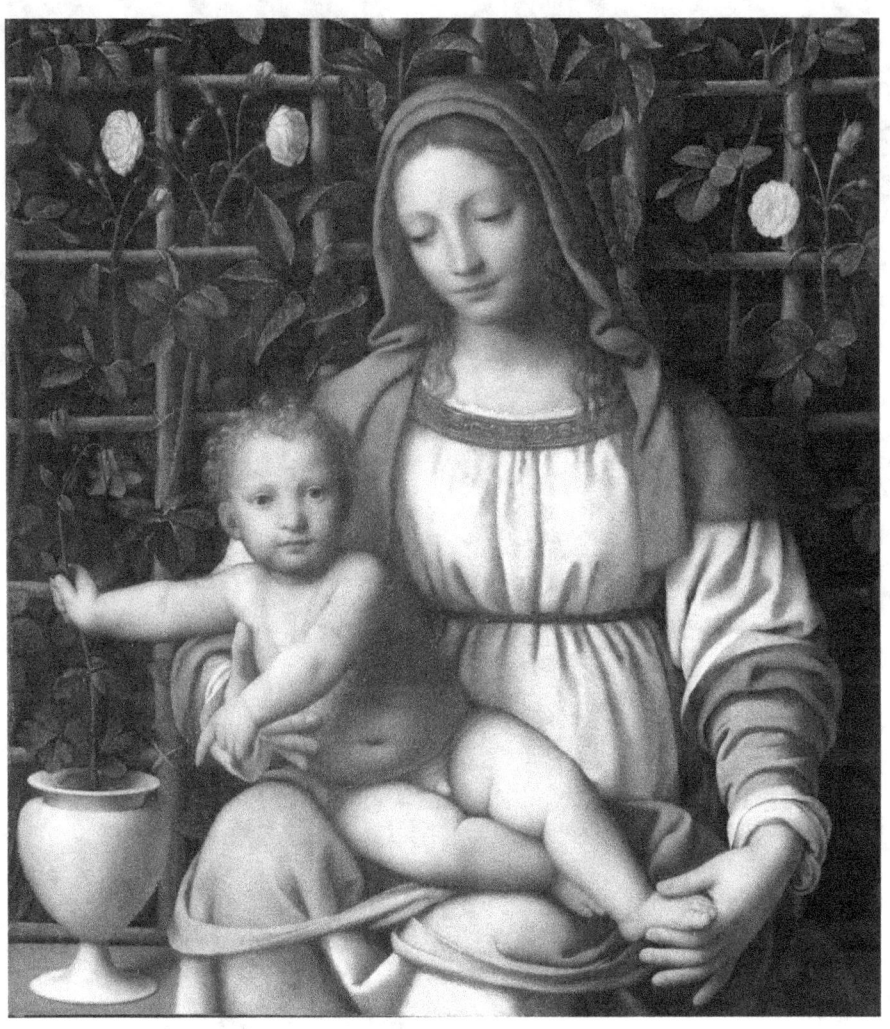

Bernardino Luini, Madonna and Child, Milan

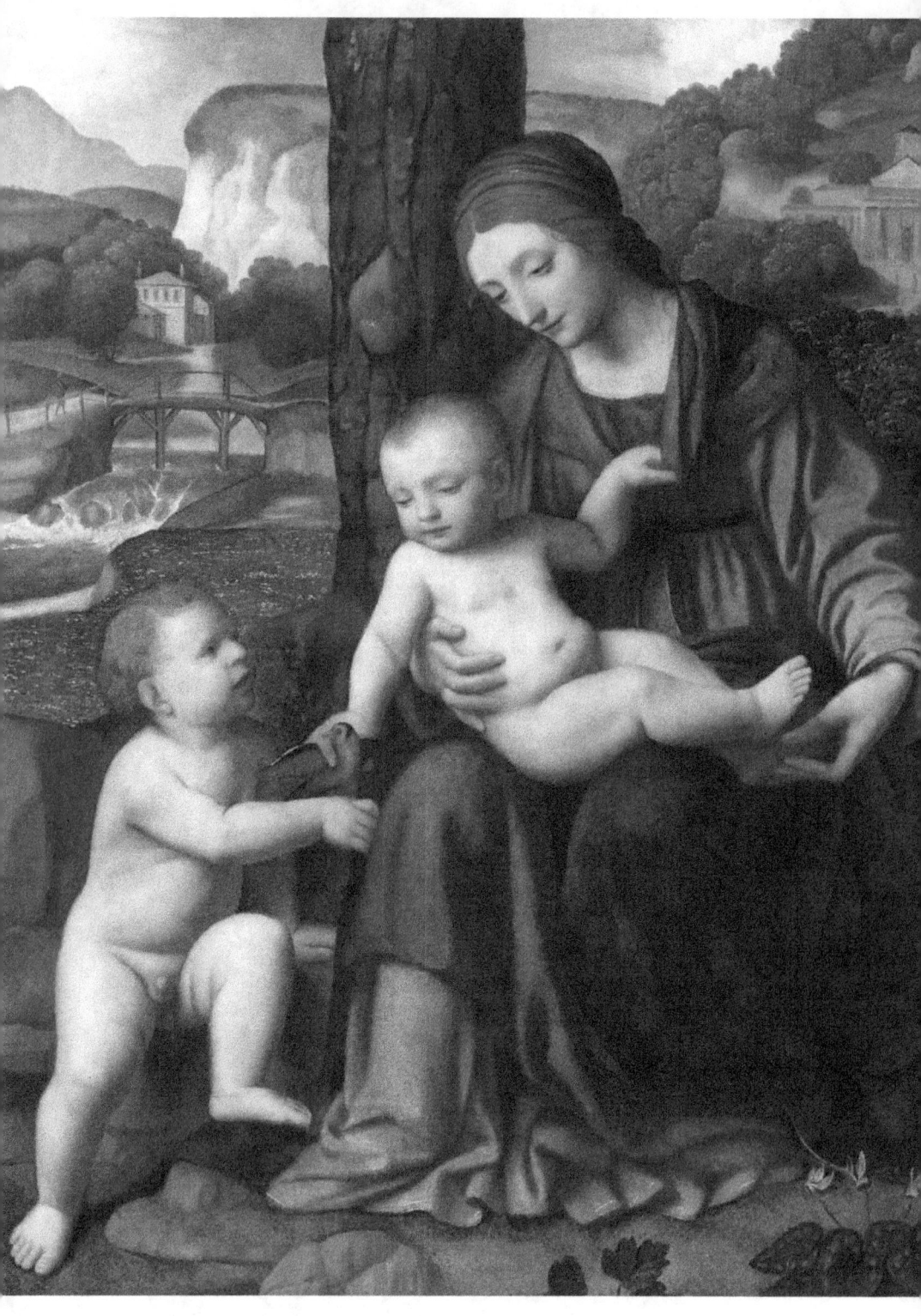

Bernardino Luini, Madonna With Child and Young St John, 1516 Vienna

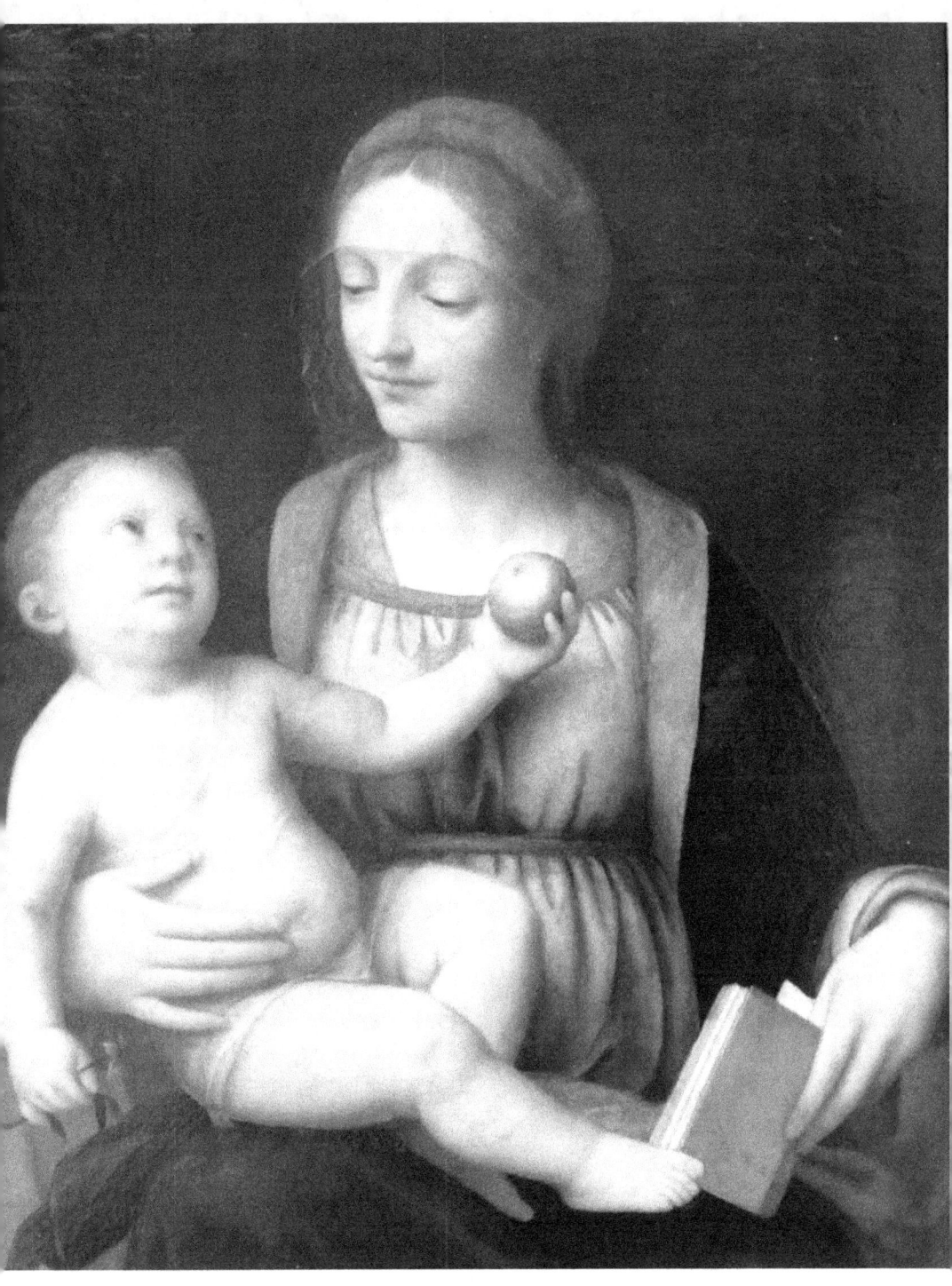

Bernardino Luini, Maria mit dem Kind und dem Apfel anagoria, Berlin

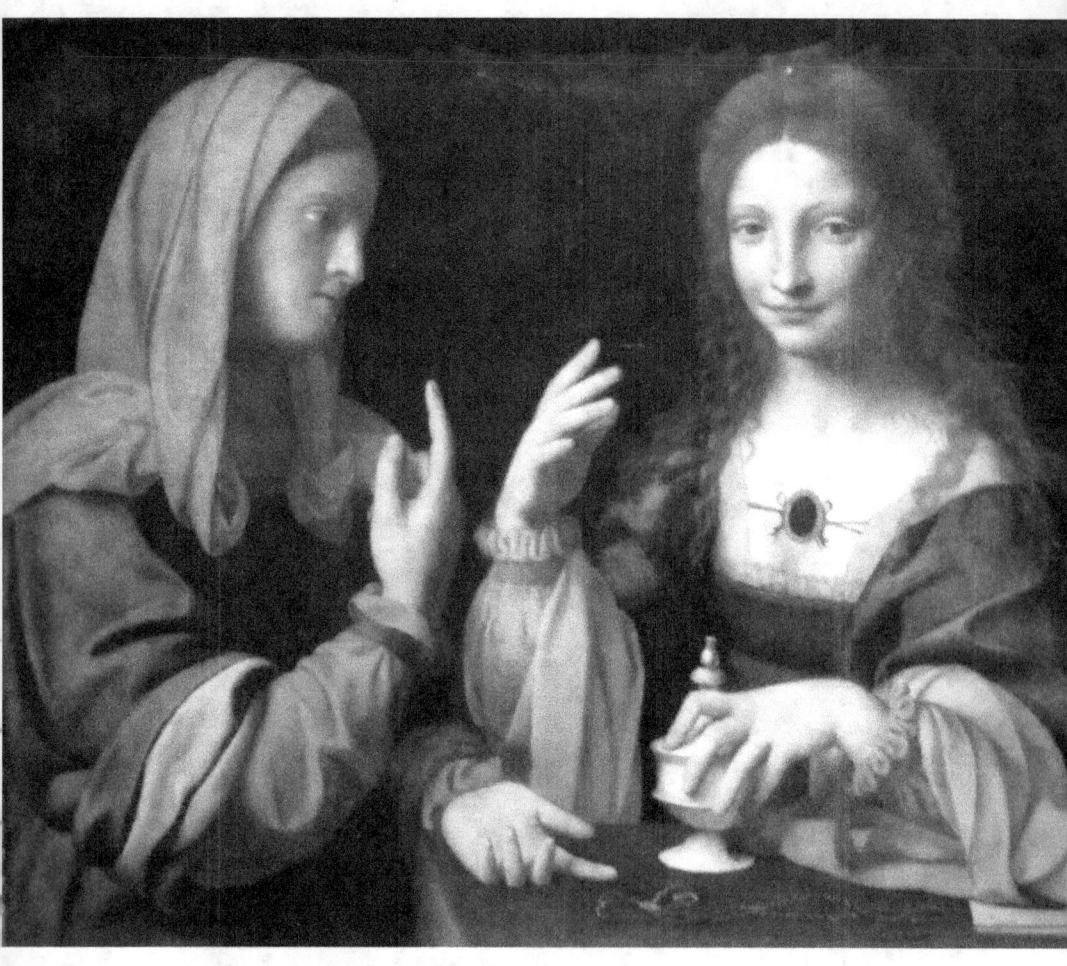

Bernardino Luini, The Conversion of the Magdalene,
or Allegory of Modesty and Vanity, 1520, San Diego

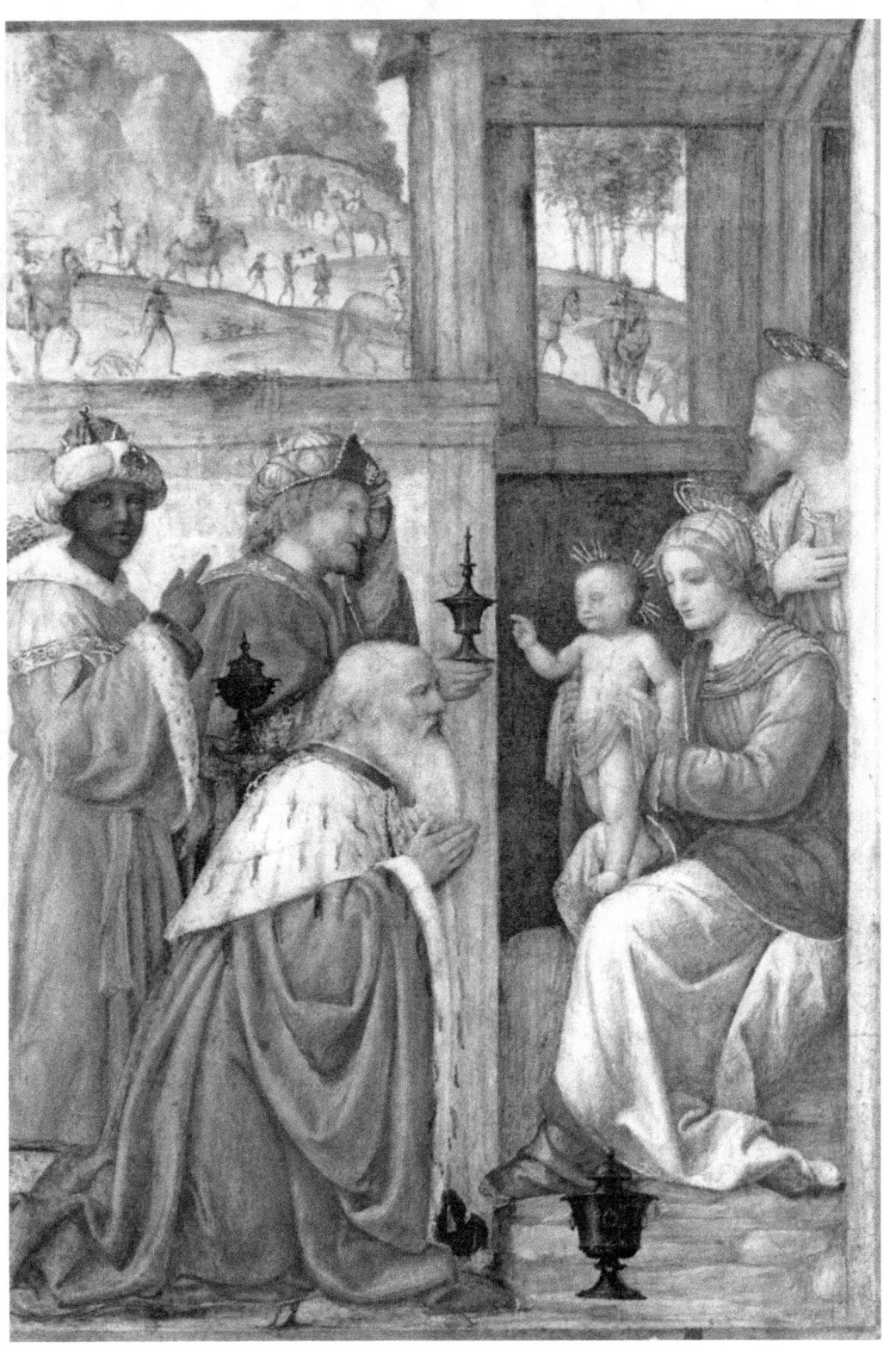

Bernardino Luini, The Adoration of the Magi, Louvre Museum

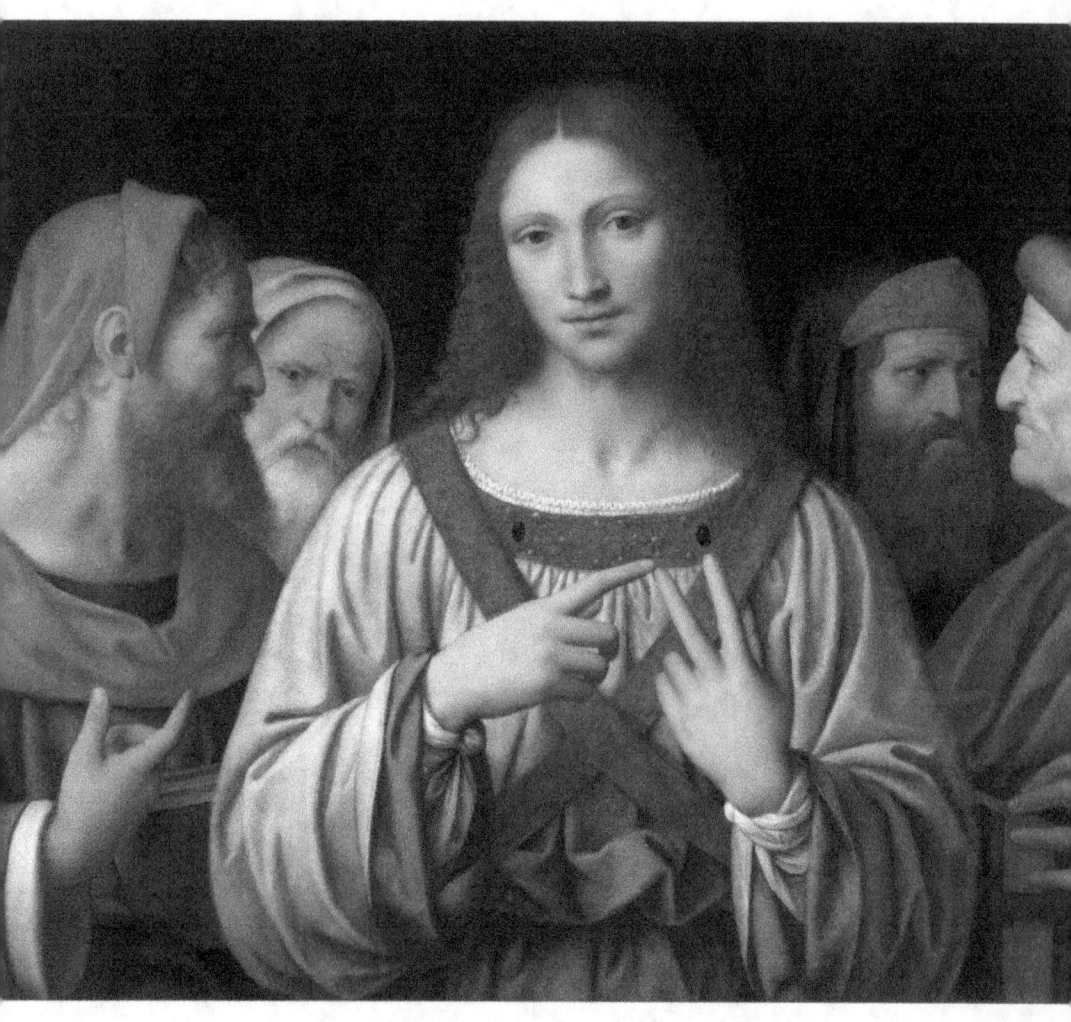

Bernardino Luini, Christ Among the Doctors, National Gallery, London

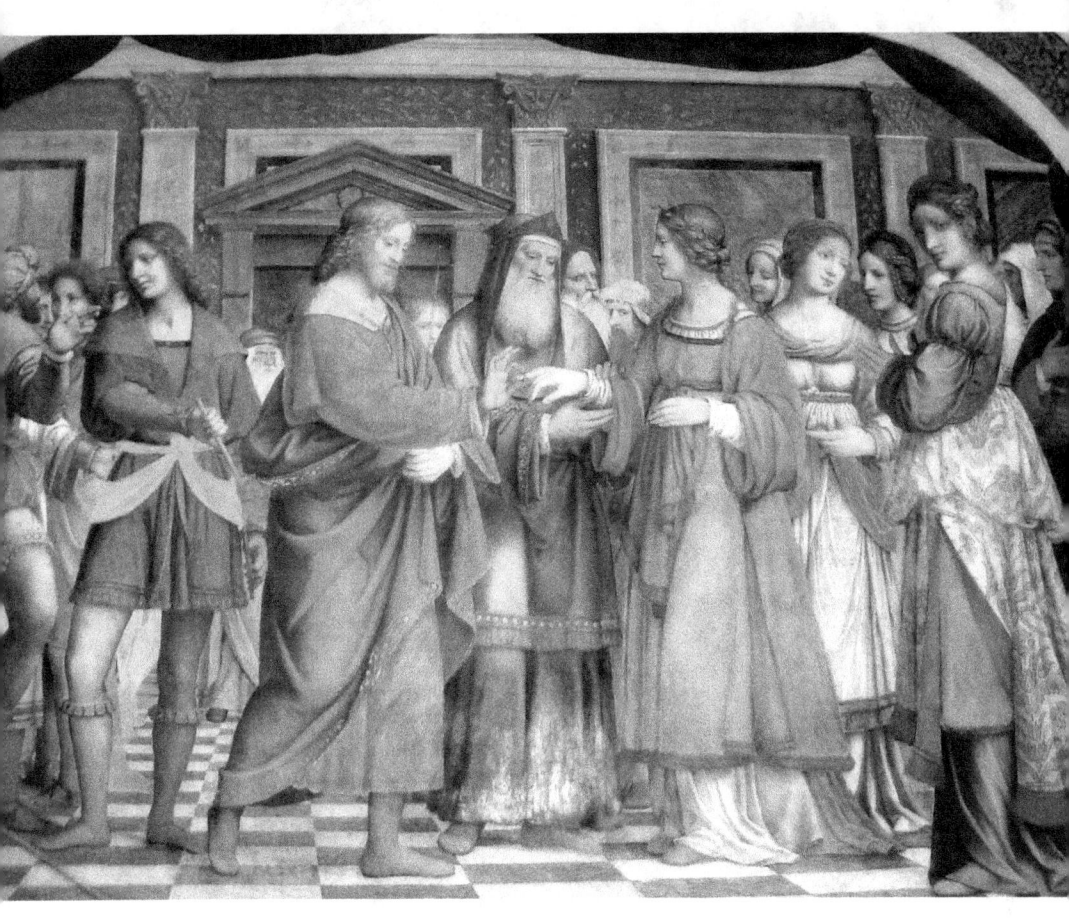

Bernardino Luini, The Engagement of Virgin Mary,
Santuario della Beata Vergine dei Miracoli, Saronno (Varese), Italy

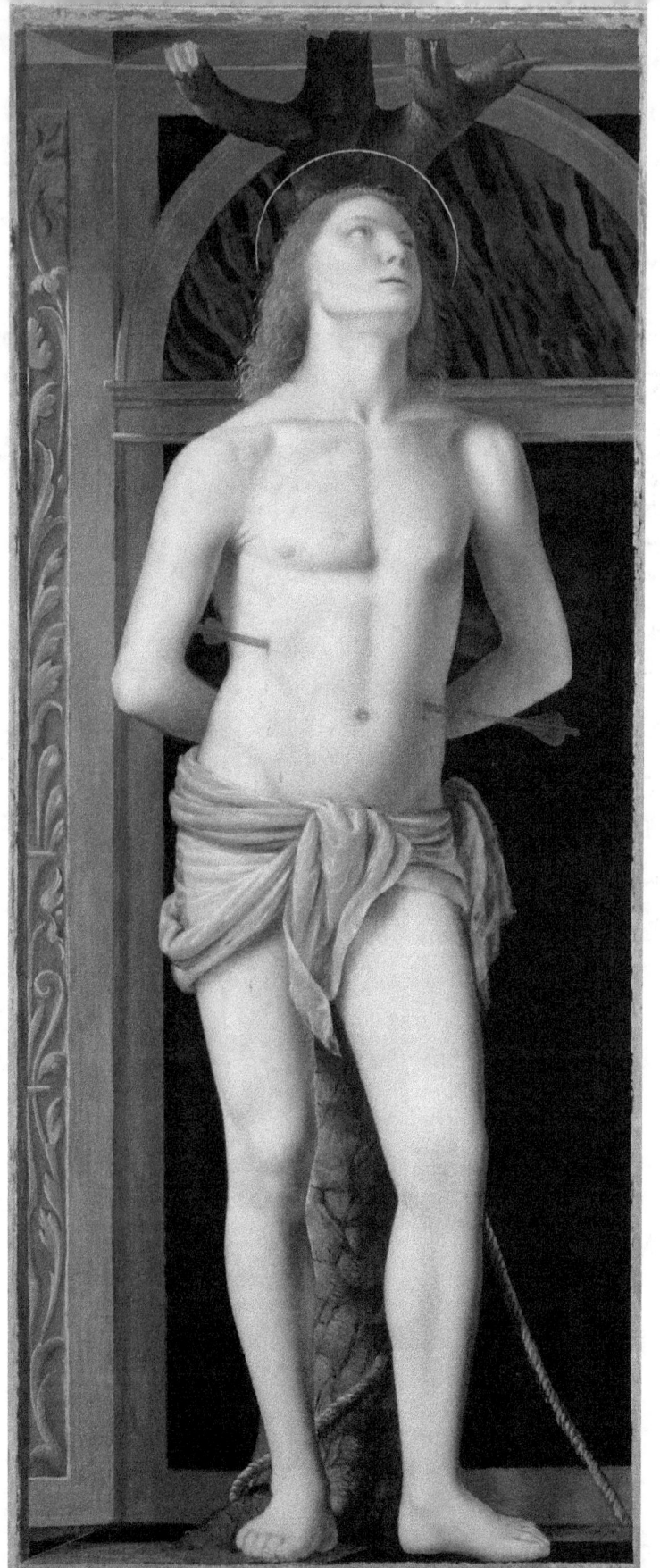

Bernardino Luini,
St Sebastian,
1520s, collection:
coll. Borromeo Isola,
Bella

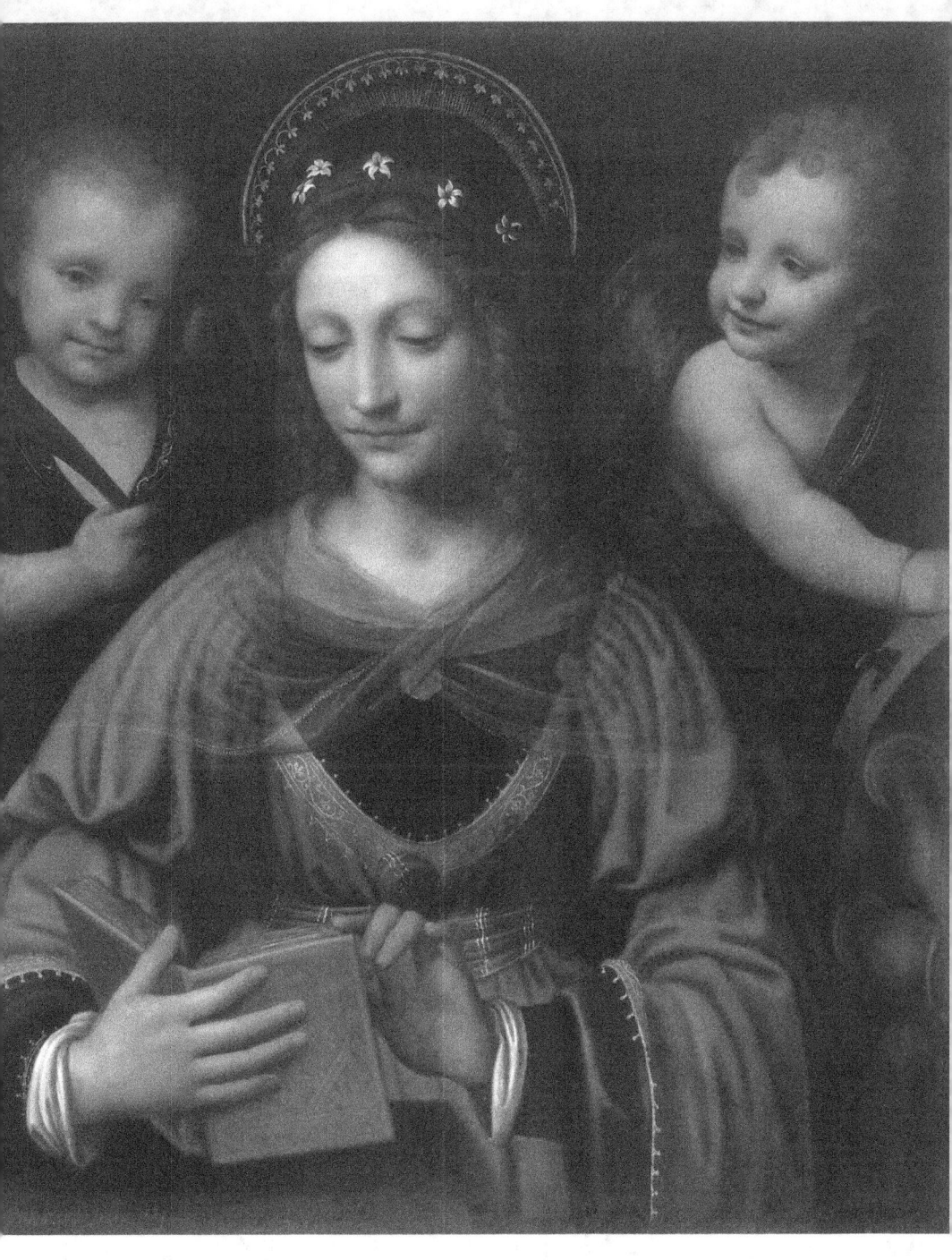

Bernardino Luini, St Catherine, 1527-31, Hermitage Museum

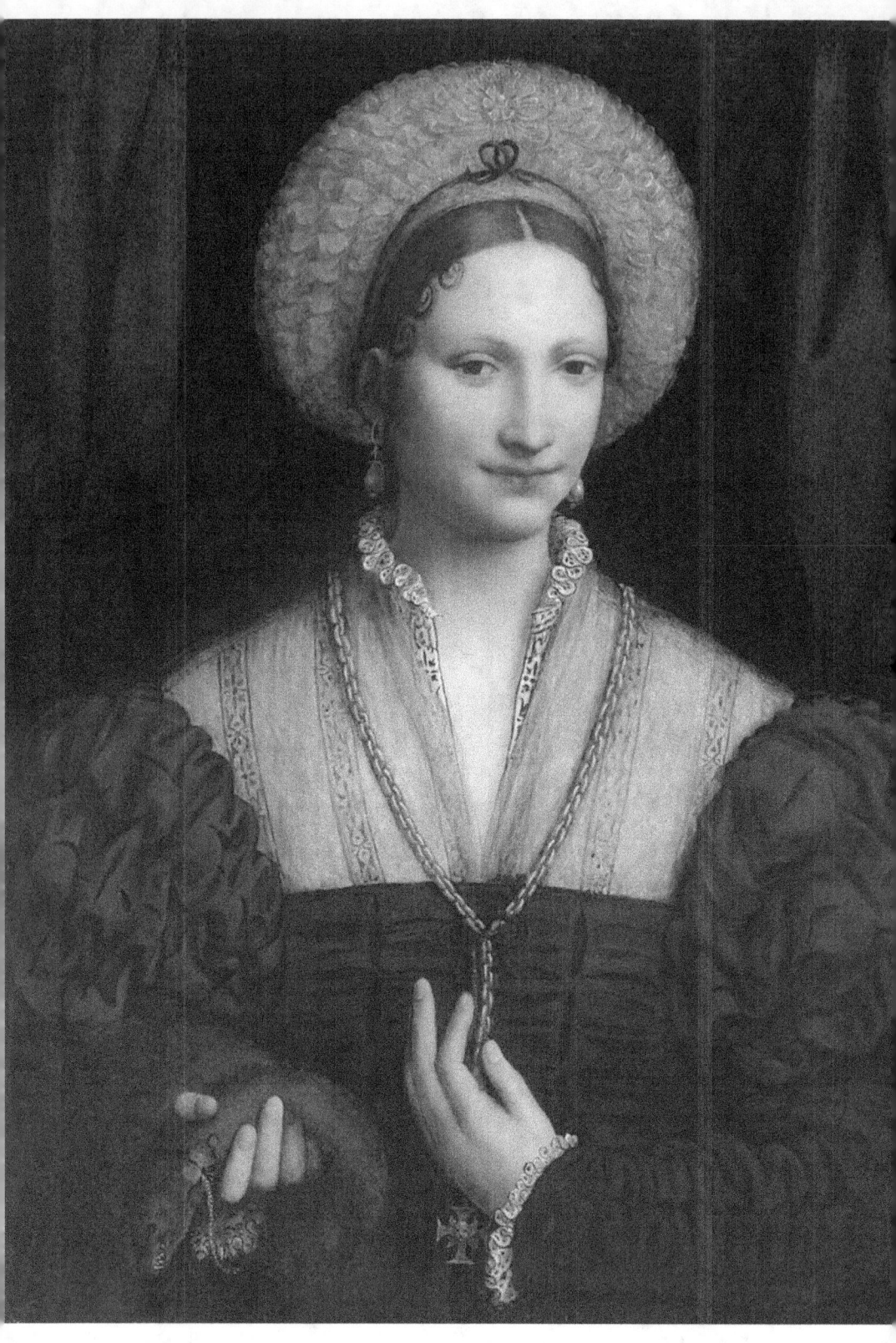

Bernardino Luini, Lady With a Flea Fur, 1520-25, Washington, DC

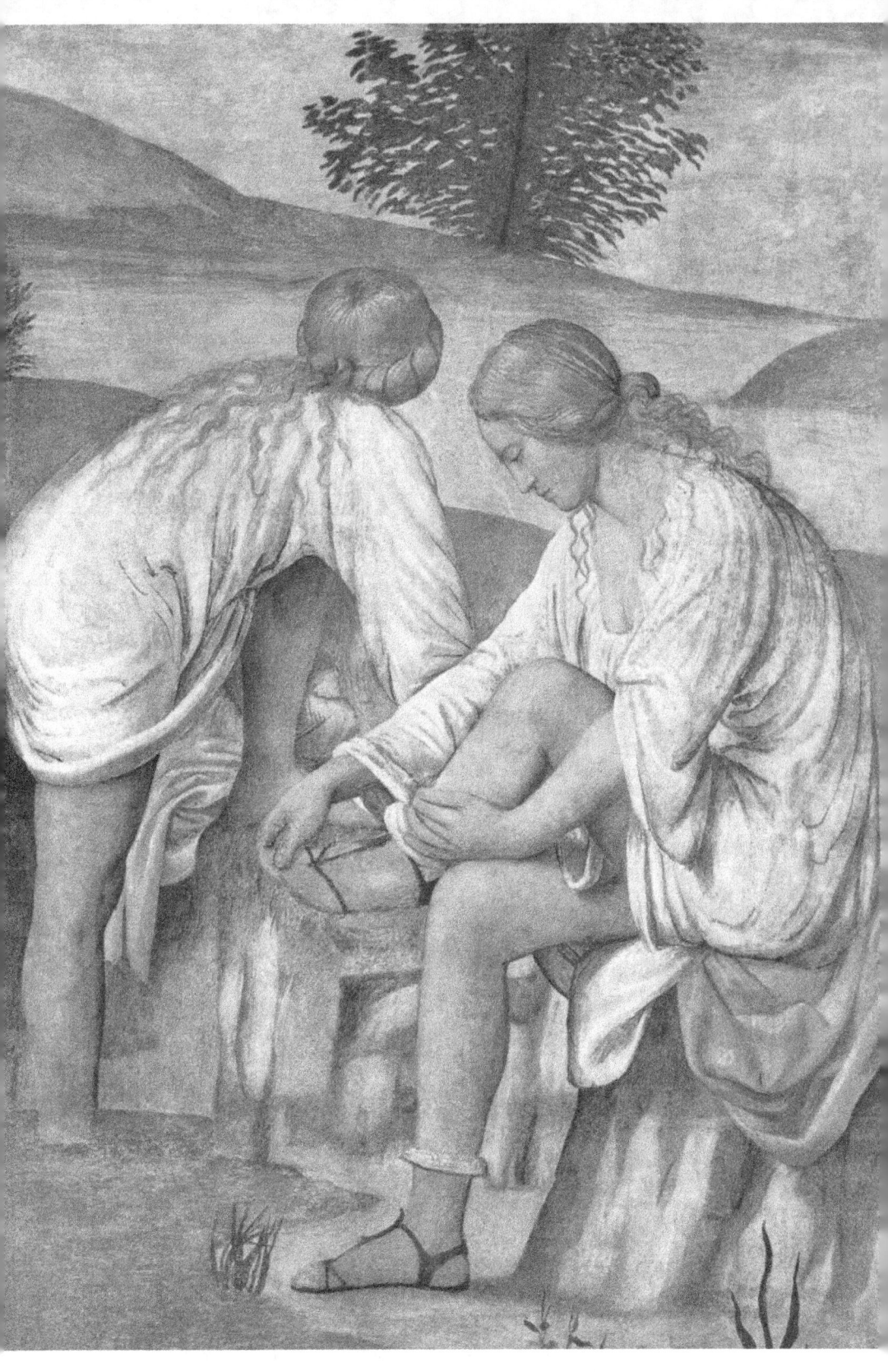

Bernardino Luini, Women Bathing, fresco, 1518, Milan

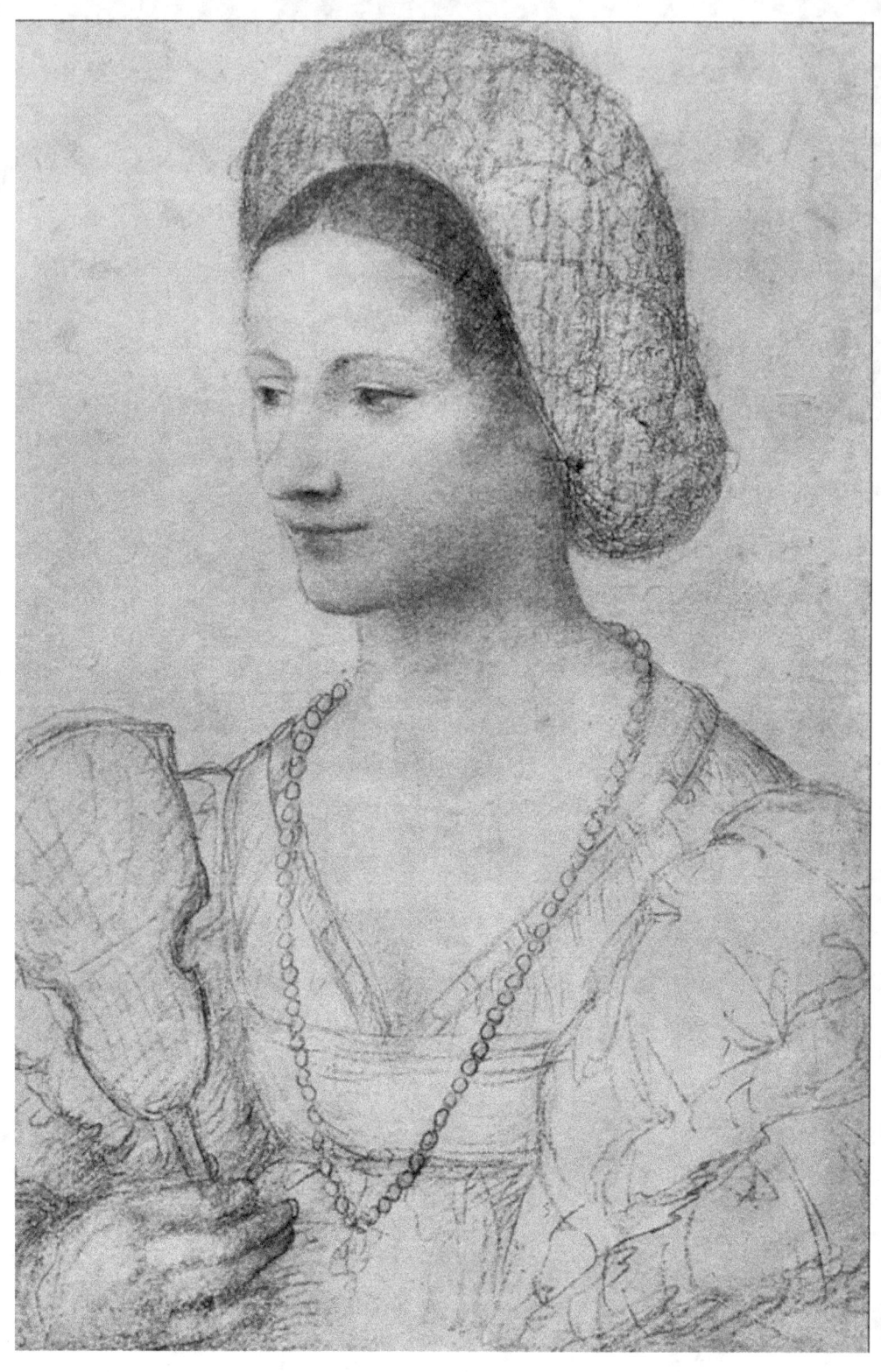

Bernardino Luini, Portrait of a Lady With a Mirror, Vienna

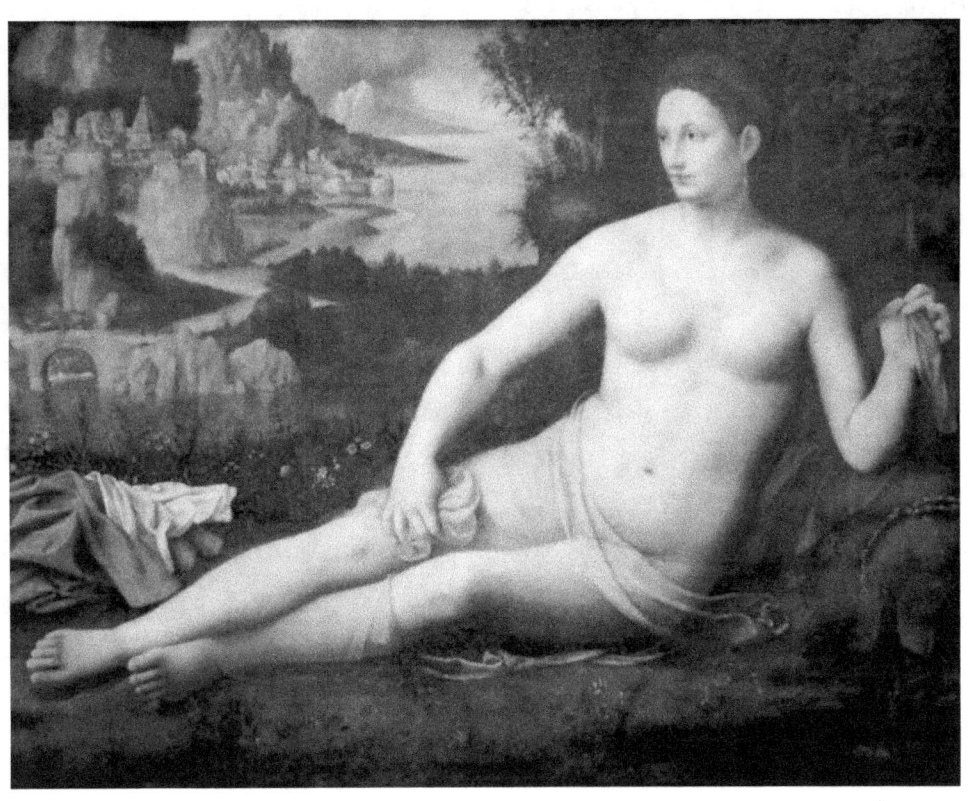

Bernardino Luini, Venus, 1530

II

As we have said already nothing is known of Luini's early life, although the fact that he was born at Luino on the Lago Maggiore seems to be beyond dispute. The people of that little lake side town have no doubt at all about the matter, and they say that the family was one of some distinction, that Giacomo of Luino who founded a monastery in his native place was the painter's uncle. Perhaps the wish was father to the thought, and because every man who sets out to study the life and work of an artist is as anxious to know as was Miss Rosa Dartle herself, there are always facts of a sort at his service. He who seeks the truth can always be supplied with something as much like it as paste is to diamonds, and can supplement the written word with the aid of tradition. The early life of the artist is a blank, and the authorities are by no means in agreement about the year of his birth. 1470 would seem to be a reasonable date, with a little latitude on either side. Many men writing long years after the painter's death, have held that he was a pupil of Leonardo da Vinci, indeed several pictures that were attributed to da Vinci by the authorities of different European galleries are now recognised as Luini's work, but the mistake is not at all difficult to explain. If we turn to "La Joconda," a portrait by da Vinci that hangs in the Louvre to-day, and is apparently beyond dispute in the eyes of the present generation of critics, and then go through the Brera in Milan with a photograph of "La Joconda's" portrait in our hand, it will be impossible to overlook the striking resemblance between Luini's types and da Vinci's smiling model. Leonardo had an academy in Milan, and it is reasonable to suppose that Luini worked in it, although at the time when he is supposed to have come for the first time to the capital of Lombardy, Leonardo da Vinci had left, apparently because Louis XII. of France, cousin and successor of that Charles VIII. who had troubled the peace of Italy for so long, was thundering at the city gates, and at such a time great artists were apt to remember that they had good patrons elsewhere. The school may, however, have remained open because no great rulers made war on artists, and Luini would have learned something of the spirit that animated Leonardo's pictures. For other masters and influence he seems to have gone to Bramantino and Foppa. Bramantino was a painter of Milan and Ambrosio Foppa known as Caradosso was a native of Pavia and should not be reckoned among Milanese artists as he has so often been. He was renowned for the beauty of his medals and his goldsmith's work; and he was one of the men employed by the great family of Bentivoglio.

It may be mentioned in this place that many Italian artists, particularly those of the Florentine schools, suffered very greatly from their unceasing devotion to the art of the miniaturist. They sought to achieve his detail, his fine but cramped handling, and this endeavour was fatal to them when they came to paint large pictures that demanded skilled composition, and the subordination of detail to a large general effect. The influence of the miniature painter and the maker of medals kept many a fifteenth-century painter in the second grade and Luini never quite survived his early devotion to their methods, often making the fatal mistake of covering a large canvas with many figures of varying size but equal value. It may be remarked that Tintoretto was the first great painter of the Renaissance who learned to subordinate parts to the whole, and he had to face a great deal of unpopularity because he saw with his own eyes instead of using those of his predecessors.

It may be suggested, with all possible respect to those who hold different opinions, that Luini, though he responded to certain influences, had no master in the generally accepted sense of the term. One cannot trace the definite relation between him and any older painter that we find between Titian and Gian Bellini, for example. He took a certain type from Leonardo, his handling from time to time recalls the other masters – we have already referred to the most important of these – but had he studied in the school of one man, had he served an apprenticeship after the fashion of his contemporaries, his pictures would surely have been free from those faults of composition and perspective that detract so much from the value of the big works. He seems to have been self-taught rather than to have been a schoolman. While his single figures are wholly admirable whether on fresco or on panel, his grouping is nearly always ineffective, one might say childish, and his sense of perspective is by no means equal to that of his greatest contemporaries. As a draughtsman and a colourist Luini had little to learn from anybody, and the poetry of his conceptions is best understood when it is remembered that he was a poet as well as a painter. He is said to have written poems and essays, though we are not in a position to say where they are to be found, and it is clear that he had a singularly detached spirit and that the hand of a skilled painter was associated with the mind of a little child. In some aspects he is as simple as those primitive painters of Umbria whose backgrounds are all of gold. Like so many other painters of the Renaissance Luini's saints and angels are peasant folk, the people he saw around him. He may have idealised them, but they remain as they were made.

A few records of the prices paid for Luini's work exist among the documents belonging to churches and religious houses, and while they justify a belief that at the time he came to Milan Luini had achieved some measure of distinction in his calling, they seem to prove that he was hardly regarded as a great painter. The prices paid to him are ridiculously small, no more than a living wage, but he had the reputation of being a reliable and painstaking artist and he would seem to have been content with a small reward for work that appealed to him. His early commissions executed in and around Milan when he first came from Luini were numerous and consisted very largely of frescoes which are the work of a young man who has not yet freed his own individuality from the influence of his elders. One of the most charming works associated with this period is the "Burial of St. Catherine," which is reproduced in these pages. The composition is simple enough, the handling does not touch the summit of the painter's later achievements, but the sentiment of the picture is quite delightful. St. Catherine is conceived in a spirit of deepest reverence and devotion, but the angels are just Lombardy peasant girls born to labour in the fields and now decorated with wings in honour of a great occasion. And yet the man who could paint this fresco and could show so unmistakably his own simple faith in the story it sets out, was a poet as well as a painter even though he had never written a line, while the treatment of his other contemporary frescoes and the fine feeling for appropriate colour suggest a great future for the artist who had not yet reached middle age. We see that Luini devoted his brush to mythological and sacred subjects, touching sacred history with a reverent hand, shutting his eyes to all that was painful, expressing all that was pitiful or calculated to strengthen the hold of religion upon the mass in fashion destined to appeal though in changing fashion for at least four centuries. Where the works have failed to triumph as expressions of a living faith they have charmed agnostics as an expression of enduring beauty.

From Milan Luini seems to have gone to Monza, a city a few miles away from the capital of Lombardy where the rulers of united Italy come after their coronation to receive the iron crown that has been worn by the kings of Lombardy for nearly a thousand years. This is the city in which the late King Umberto, that brave and good man, was foully murdered by an anarchist. To-day one reaches Monza by the help of a steam-tram that blunders heavily enough over the wide flat Lombardy plain. The Milanese go to Monza for the sake of an outing, but most of the tourists who throng the city stay away, and it is possible to spend a few pleasant hours in the cathedral and churches with never a flutter of red-covered guide book to distract one's attention from the matters to which the hasty tourist is blind. Here Luini painted frescoes, and it is known that he stayed for a long time at the house of one of the strong men of Monza and painted a large number of frescoes there. To-day the fortress, if it was one, has become a farmhouse, and the frescoes, more than a dozen in all, have been taken away to the Royal Palace in Milan. Dr. Williamson in his interesting volume to which the student of Luini must be deeply indebted, says that there is one left at the Casa Pelucca. The writer in the course of two days spent in Monza was unfortunate enough to overlook it.

It has been stated that the facts relating to Luini's life are few and far between. Fiction on the other hand is plentiful, and there is a story that Luini, shortly after his arrival in Milan, was held responsible by the populace for the death of a priest who fell from a hastily erected scaffolding in the church of San Giorgio where the artist was working. The rest of the legend follows familiar lines that would serve the life story of any leading artist of the time, seeing that they all painted altar-pieces and used scaffolding. He is said to have fled to Monza, to have been received by the chief of the Pelucca family, to have paid for his protection with the frescoes that have now been brought from Monza to the Brera, to have fallen violently in love with the beautiful daughter of the house, to have engaged in heroic contests against great odds on her behalf, and so on, *ad absurdum*. If we look at the portraits the painter is said to have made of himself and to have placed in pictures at Saronna and elsewhere we shall see that Luini was hardly the type of man to have engaged in the idle pursuits of chivalry in the intervals of the work to which his life was given. We have the head of a man of thought not that of a man of action, and all the character of the face gives the lie to the suggestions of the storytellers. It is clear, however, that the painter made a long stay in Monza and when he came back to Milan he worked for the churches of St. Maurizio, Santa Maria della Pace, Santa Maria di Brera, and St. Ambrosia.

In Milan he found a great patron, no less a man than Giovanni Bentivoglio who had been driven from his rule over Bologna by the "Terrible Pontiff" Julius II., that life-long opponent and bitter enemy of the Borgia Pope Alexander VI. Alessandro Bentivoglio, the son of the ruined Giovanni, married Ippolita Sforza, daughter of one of the house that had done so much to rule Rome until Pope Alexander VI. broke its power. Alessandro Bentivoglio commissioned Luini to paint altar-pieces in St. Maurizio where his father was buried, and the painter included in his work a portrait of Ippolita Sforza with three female saints. He did much other work in this church; some of it has faded almost beyond recognition.

At the same time there is no need to think that we have recovered the last work of Luini or indeed of the great masters even in the churches of Italy. Only a few months ago the writer was in a small Italian church that had suffered a few years ago from disastrous floods. The water unable to find no outlet had risen for a time almost to the top of the supporting columns. The smooth wall above was plastered, and when the waters had subsided it was found that the plaster had become so damaged that it was necessary to remove it. Happily the work was done carefully, for under the whitewash some excellent frescoes were discovered. They would seem to have profited by their covering for as much as has been uncovered is rich and well preserved. It may be that in days when the State of Italy was seriously disturbed, and Napoleon, greatest of highwaymen and conquerors, after being crowned in Milan with the famous Monza crown, was laying his hand on all that seemed worth carrying away, some one in authority thought of this simple method of concealment, and obtained expert advice that enabled the frescoes to be covered without serious damage. Under similar conditions we may yet discover some of the earlier work of Luini, because it is clear that the years in which his reputation was in the making must have been full of achievement of which the greater part has now been lost. He could hardly have been less than thirty years of age when he came to Milan with a reputation sufficient to gain commissions for work in churches; that reputation must have taken years to acquire, and must have been associated with very definite accomplishment. The lack of all record was essentially the misfortune that beset men who were not very high in the esteem of their contemporaries. A painter like Luini would have executed a great many pictures for people who could not pay very well, and had no great gallery or well-built church to harbour the work, and in the course of time the work would tend inevitably to disappear before the devouring candle-smoke, or to be carried away by unscrupulous purchasers who chanced to be better equipped with taste than conscience. On the other hand, painters who led the various movements of their time would be honoured by successive generations and their work would be stored in the best and safest places. To be sure, fire was never a respecter of palaces or persons, and the flames have consumed more work than a collection of the finest Renaissance pictures in existence could show, but even then the odds seem to be in favour of the bigger men because special efforts would be made to save their paintings while those of lesser men would be left with few regrets to take their chance.

When Luini was engaged to work in the Church of St. Maurizio there was a fair chance that his altar-pieces and frescoes would be well looked after, but when he worked for a small provincial family like the Pelucca the house sank with the family fortunes till at last it became a farm, and in the early years of the nineteenth century the frescoes were taken from the walls with as much care as was deemed advisable. Doubtless Luini worked for many men whose worldly position was not as considerable as that of the Pelucca family, and that work may have disappeared altogether. The painter, as we have seen, did not enjoy the patronage of many great men before Alessandro Bentivoglio, and large institutions were not numbered among his early clients. But he was not altogether without valuable patronage in the latter days, and in the early 'twenties of the sixteenth century the influential Brotherhood of the Holy Crown, one of the leading charitable institutions of Milan, would seem to have given him some official connection with their institution; a recognised position without fixed salary. For them he painted the magnificent frescoes now in the Ambrosian Library. The great work there was divided by the artist into three parts separated by pillars. In the centre Luini has depicted the crowning with thorns, Christ being seated upon a throne while thorns are being put upon His head; His arms are crossed; His expression one of supreme resignation. Above Him little angels look down or point to a cartouche on which is written "Caput Regis Gloriæ Spinis Coranatur." In the left hand division of the fresco and on the right, the fore-ground is filled with kneeling figures whose heads are supposed to be portraits of the most prominent members of the Society. Clearly they are all men who have achieved some measure of honour and distinction. Above the kneeling figures on the left hand side St. John is pointing out the tragedy of the central picture to the Virgin Mary, while on the right hand side a man in armour and another who is seen faintly behind him call the attention of a third to what is happening. A crown of thorns hangs above the right and the left hand compartment and there is a landscape for background. It is recorded that this work took about six months, and was finished in March 1522 at a cost to the Society of 115 soldi. So Luini's work looks down to-day upon a part of the great Ambrosian Library, and it may well be that the library itself will yield to patient investigation some record, however simple, of the painter's life, sufficient perhaps to enable us to readjust our mental focus and see his lovable figure more clearly.

It may be urged that for those of us who are content to see with the spiritual eye Luini is expressed more eloquently by his work, and particularly by this great picture in the Ambrosian

Library, than he could hope to be by the combined efforts of half-a-dozen critics, each with his own special point of view and his properly profound contempt for the views of others. The painter's low tones and subtle harmonies, his pure but limited vision, speak to us of a gentle, refined, and delicate nature, of an achievement that stopped short of cleverness and consequently limited him to the quieter byways of artistic life, while those whose inspiration was less, and whose gifts were more, moved with much pomp and circumstance before admiring contemporaries. The refined mind, the sensitive soul, shrank from depicting the tragedy of the Crown of Thorns in the realistic fashion that would have proved acceptable to so many other artists. Luini forgets the blood and the spikes, he almost forgets the physical pain, and gives us the Man of Sorrows who has forgiven His tormentors because "they know not what they do."

Continental galleries show us many treatments of the same familiar theme, they have none to show that can vie with this in a combination of strength and delicacy that sets out an immortal story while avoiding the brutal realism to which so many other artists have succumbed. We may suppose that the objects of the Society roused Luini's sympathy to an extent that made it easy for him to accept the somewhat paltry remuneration with which the Brotherhood of the Holy Crown rewarded him, and so the picture makes its own appeal on the painter's behalf, and tells a story of his claims upon our regard. A man may lie, in fact it may be suggested on the strength of the Psalmist's statement that most men do, but an artist's life work tells his story in spite of himself, and if he labour with pen or brush his truest biography will be seen in what he leaves behind him. It is not possible to play a part throughout all the vicissitudes of a long career, and no man could have given us the pictures that Luini has left unless he chanced to be a choice and rare spirit. We may remember here and now that the time was richer in violent contrasts than any of its successors, the most deplorable excesses on the one hand, the most rigid virtues on the other, seem to have been the special product of the Renaissance. While there were men who practised every vice under the sun there were others who sought to arrest Divine Retribution by the pursuit of all the virtues, and while the progress of the years has to a certain extent made men neutral tinted in character, the season of the Renaissance was one of violent contrasts. On behalf of the section that went in pursuit of righteousness let it be remembered that heaven and the saints were not matters for speculation, they were certainties. Every man knew that God was in heaven, and that if the workers of iniquity flourished, it was that they might be destroyed for ever. Every man knew that the saints still exerted their supernatural powers and would come down to earth if need be to protect a devotee. Satan, on the other hand, went armed about the earth seeking whom he might devour, and hell was as firmly fixed as heaven. In order to understand Luini, his life and times, these facts must be borne in mind. The greater the unrest in the cities the more the public attention would be turned to statesmen and warriors, and when the personalities of artists began to be considered, those who lived and thrived in the entourage of popes and rulers monopolised the attention. Hundreds of men were at work earning a fair living and some local repute, it was left to foreign favour to set a seal upon success. Had Luini chanced to be invited to Venice or to Rome he would have been honoured throughout Lombardy; but a painter like a prophet is often without honour in his own country. Luini's gifts were of a more quiet and domestic order than those of his great contemporaries Leonardo da Vinci and Michelangelo, for example, were more than painters, and perhaps it was only in Venice that painting stood by itself and managed to thrive alone. Luini would have come into his kingdom while he lived had Venice been his birthplace. The genius of the Florentine school sought to express itself in half-a-dozen different ways, no triumph in one department of work could satisfy men whose longing for self-expression was insatiable. In those days it was possible for a man to make himself master of all knowledge, literally he could discourse *de omnibus rebus et quibusdam aliis.* And this diffusion of interests was fatal to many a genius that might have moved to amazing triumph along one road.

It is clear that Bernardino Luini never travelled very far from his native country either physically or mentally. In the eyes of his contemporaries he was not a man of sufficient importance to receive commissions from the great art centres of Italy. This, of course, may be because he did not have the good fortune to attract the attention of the connoisseurs of his day, for we find that outside Milan, and the little town of Luino where he was born and whence he took his name, his work was done in comparatively small towns like Como, Legnano, Lugano, Ponte, and Saronno. Milan and Monza may be disregarded because we have already dealt with the work there. Saronno, which lies some fourteen miles north-west of Milan, is little more than a village to-day, and its chief claim upon the attention of the traveller is its excellent gingerbread for which it is famous throughout Lombardy. It has a celebrated church known as the Sanctuary of the Blessed Virgin and here one finds some very fine examples of our painter's frescoes. Some of the frescoes in the church are painted by Cesare del Magno others by Lanini, and the rest are from the hand of Bernardino Luini. Round these frescoes, which are of abiding beauty, and include fine studies of the great plague saint, St. Roque, and that very popular martyr St. Sebastian, many legends congregate. It is said that Luini having killed a man in a brawl fled from Milan to the Church of the Blessed Virgin in Monza to claim sanctuary at the hand of the monks. They gave him the refuge he demanded, and, says the legend, he paid for it with frescoes. This is little more than a variant of the story that he went to Monza under similar circumstances and obtained the protection of the Pelucca family on the same terms. In the absence of anything in the nature of reliable record this story has been able to pass, but against it one likes to put the tradition that one of the heads in the frescoes is that of Luini himself. We find that head so simple, so refined, and so old – the beard is long and the hair is scanty – and so serene in its expression that it is exceedingly difficult to believe that brawling could have entered into the artist's life.

The subjects of the pictures in Saronno's Sanctuary are all biblical. We have an Adoration of the Magi, showing the same muddled composition that detracts from the other merits of the artist's work; a beautiful Presentation in the Temple in which the composition is a great deal better; and a perfectly delightful Nativity. There is a Christ is Disputing with the Doctors, and this is the picture in which we find the head that is said to be a portrait of the painter himself. Two female saints figure in another picture, and Luini's favourites St. Roque and St. Sebastian are not forgotten. Certainly if the monks obtained all that work at the price of the painter's safety they were very fortunate in his choice of sanctuary.

Como is, of course, a more important town with large industries and important factories, and one of the finest cathedrals in northern Italy. For the interior Luini painted another Adoration of the Magi and another of his favourite Nativities. It is not easy to speak about the conditions under which this work was done, and the inhabitants have so many more profitable matters to attend to that they do not seem to trouble themselves about the history of the painter who helped to make their beautiful cathedral still more beautiful.

Legnano, with its memories of Frederick Barbarossa, is within twenty miles of Milan, and for the Church of San Magno Luini painted one of his finest altar-pieces. It is in seven divisions and has earned as much critical admiration as any work from the master's brush.

Lugano is of course in Switzerland, well across the Italian border. It is a popular place enough to-day, and so far as we can tell, it was the city in which Luini painted his last pictures. He must have left Milan about 1528 or 1529, and he would seem to have gone there to execute commissions, for in the Church of Santa Maria degli Angioli we find some of his latest and finest work. The Crucifixion and the Passion, on the wall of the screen, contains several hundred figures arranged in lines in most archaic fashion. At first sight the work appears as a mere mass of figures without any central point in the composition, and with very little relief for the eye of the spectator who may come to the church surfeited with the bewildering riches of many Italian galleries. But for those who will take the trouble to study the details of this fine work there is very much to admire. In the scene of the picture Christ is seen on the cross surrounded by angels. On his right hand the penitent thief on the cross is guarded by an angel, while on the left the impenitent one is watched by a devil with a curly tail and spiked wings. Below in perfectly bewildering fashion are many figures that may be recognised with little effort – Mary Magdalen, the Madonna, Joseph of Arimathæa, Roman soldiers, some of the general public – a confused crowd. The whole picture is supported by figures of San Sebastian and St. Roque seen on either side of the arch. Stories from the life of Christ are depicted in the upper parts of the picture, all are painted with the skill of a great artist and the fervour of a devotee, but the arrangement is hopelessly confused. Luini also painted a "Last Supper" for this church and a "Madonna with the Infant Christ and St. John." This is signed "Bernardino Luini, anno 1530." From 1530 until 1533 the career of the artist cannot be traced, but in 1533 he was in Lugano again, and after that year he passes altogether from our sight. Stray writers mention his name, some venture to carry the date of his life into the 'forties, but we have no proof save their word, no work to record the later years, and all our conjecture is vain. It must suffice for us that Luini's life as far as his art was concerned ends for us with the year 1533. If he lived and worked after that date the facts relating to the following years and the work done in the latter days are left for future students to discover. It is well to remember that the Saronno portrait makes the painter look much older than he is supposed to have been.

To his contemporaries it is clear that Luini was a man of small importance. His best work is seen outside the radius of the great

Art centres of Italy, and it was only when he attracted the attention of great critics and sound judges like Morelli, John Ruskin, and John Addington Symonds that the lovers of beautiful pictures began to go out of their way to find his best work in the little towns whose churchmen were his patrons. So many of the lesser men had all his faults – that is to say, lack of perspective and inability to compose a big picture – that he was classed with them by those critics whose special gift lies in the discovery of faults. The qualities that make the most enduring appeal to us to-day were those that were least likely to make a strong impression upon the strenuous age of physical force in which he lived. When great conquerors and men who had accomplished all that force could achieve felt themselves at liberty to turn to prolonged consideration of the other sides of life they employed other masters. Then as now there were fashions in painters. The men for whom Luini strove were of comparatively small importance. A conqueror could have gathered up in the hollow of his hand all the cities, Milan excepted, in which Luini worked throughout his well-spent life, and in the stress and strife of the later years when great pictures did change hands from time to time by conquest, Luini's panel pictures in the little cities of his labours passed quite unnoticed, while even if the frescoes were admired it was not easy to move them. When at last his undoubted merits began to attract attention of connoisseurs, these connoisseurs were wondering why Leonardo da Vinci had left such a small number of pictures. They found work that bore a great resemblance to Leonardo and they promptly claimed that they had discovered the lost masterpieces. Consequently Leonardo received the credit that was due to the man who may have worked in his Milanese school and was undoubtedly under his influence for a time. And many of the beautiful panel pictures that show Luini at his best were attributed to Leonardo until nineteenth-century criticism proved competent enough to render praise where it was due, and to say definitely and with firm conviction that the unknown painter from Luino, who lived sometime between 1470 and 1540, was the true author.

If, in dealing with the life of Bernardino Luini, we are forced to content ourselves with meagre scraps of biography and little details that would have no importance at all in dealing with a life that was traceable from early days to its conclusion, it is well to remember that the most important part of the great artist is his work. Beethoven's nine symphonies, Milton's "Paradise Lost," the landscapes of Corot, the portraits of Velazquez, and the carving of Grinling Gibbons are not more precious to us because we know something of the life of the men who did the work. Nor are the "Iliad" and the fragments that remain of the works of the great Greek sculptors less to us because a shadowy tradition is all that surrounds the lives of the men who gave immortal work to the world. We must remember that it is as difficult to deal with art in terms of literature as it is to express the subtle charm of music in words. Had Luini's years boasted or regretted a series of gossiping newspapers we should have gathered a rich harvest of fact, but the facts would have left the painter where he is. There is enough of Luini left in Milan and the smaller places we have named to tell us what the man was and the spirit in which he worked, and while we will welcome the new-comer who can add to our scanty store of authenticated facts we can hardly expect that they will deepen our admiration of work that for all its shortcomings must be remembered when we turn to ponder the greatest achievements of Italian Art. It forms "a magic speculum, much gone to rust, indeed, yet in fragments still clear; wherein the marvellous image of his existence does still shadow itself, though fitfully, and as with an intermittent light."

On the following pages are some contemporaries of Luini.

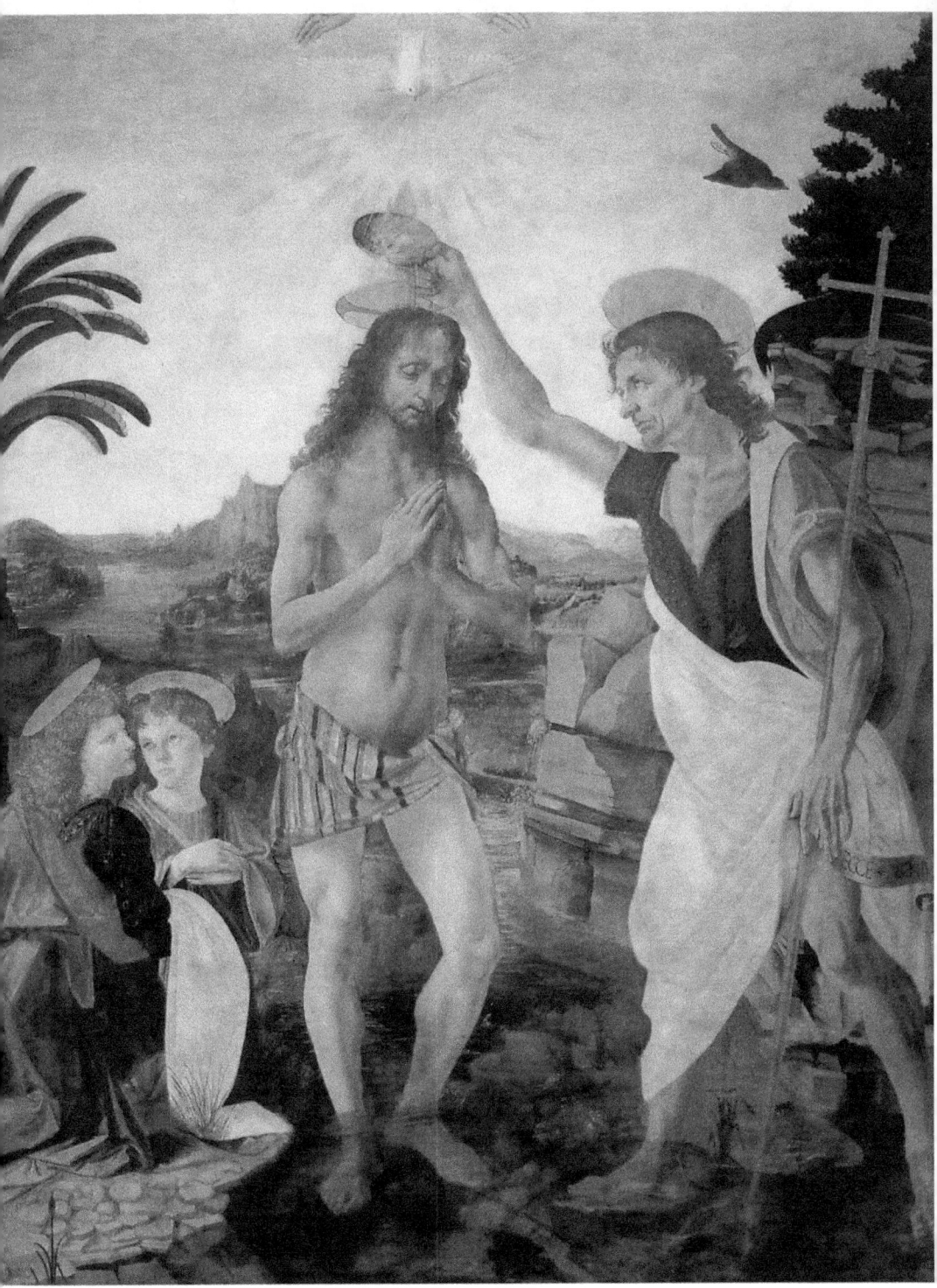

Andrea del Verrocchio, The Baptism of Christ

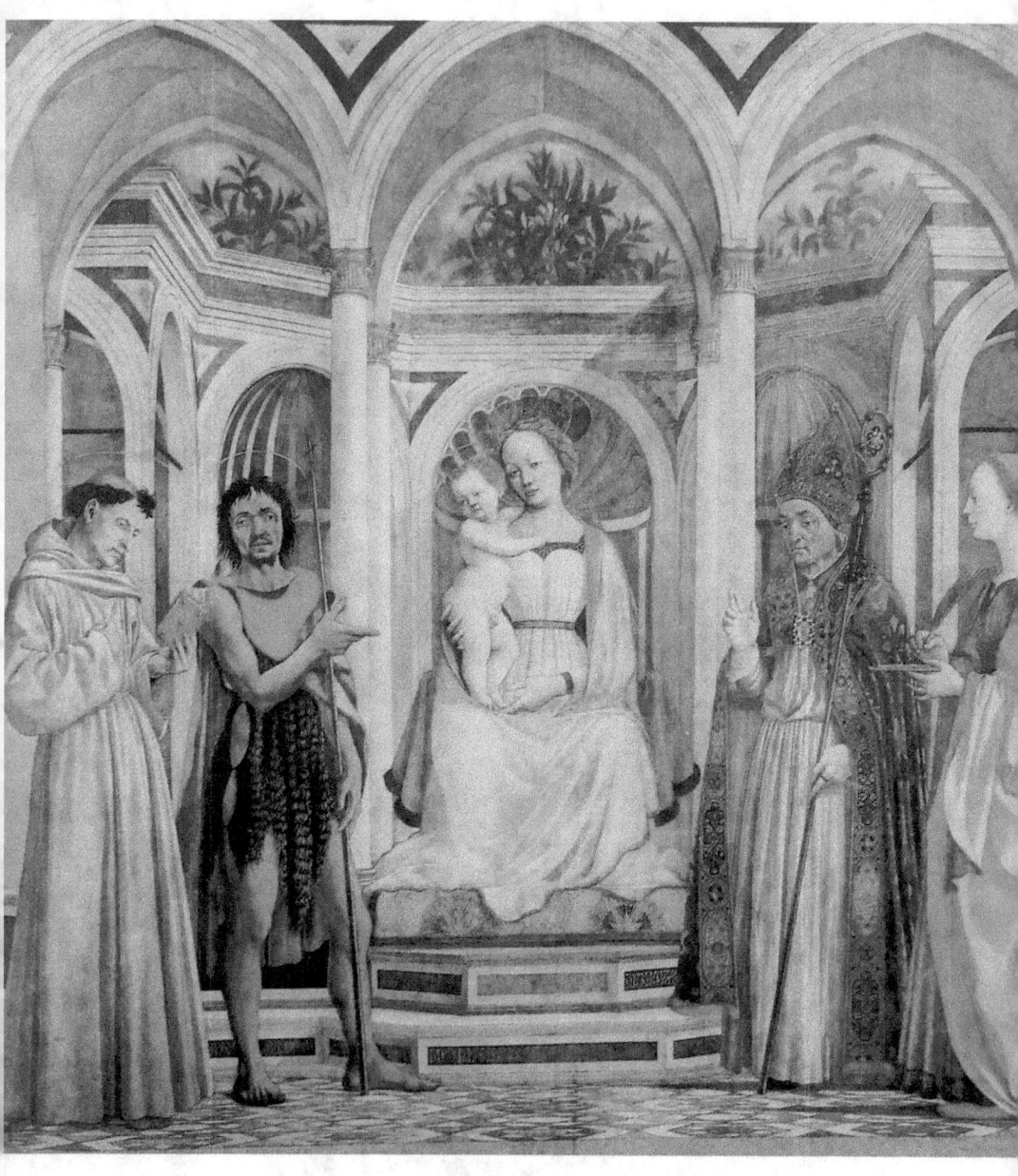

Domenico Veneziano, Madonna and Child With Saints, 1445, Uffizi Gallery

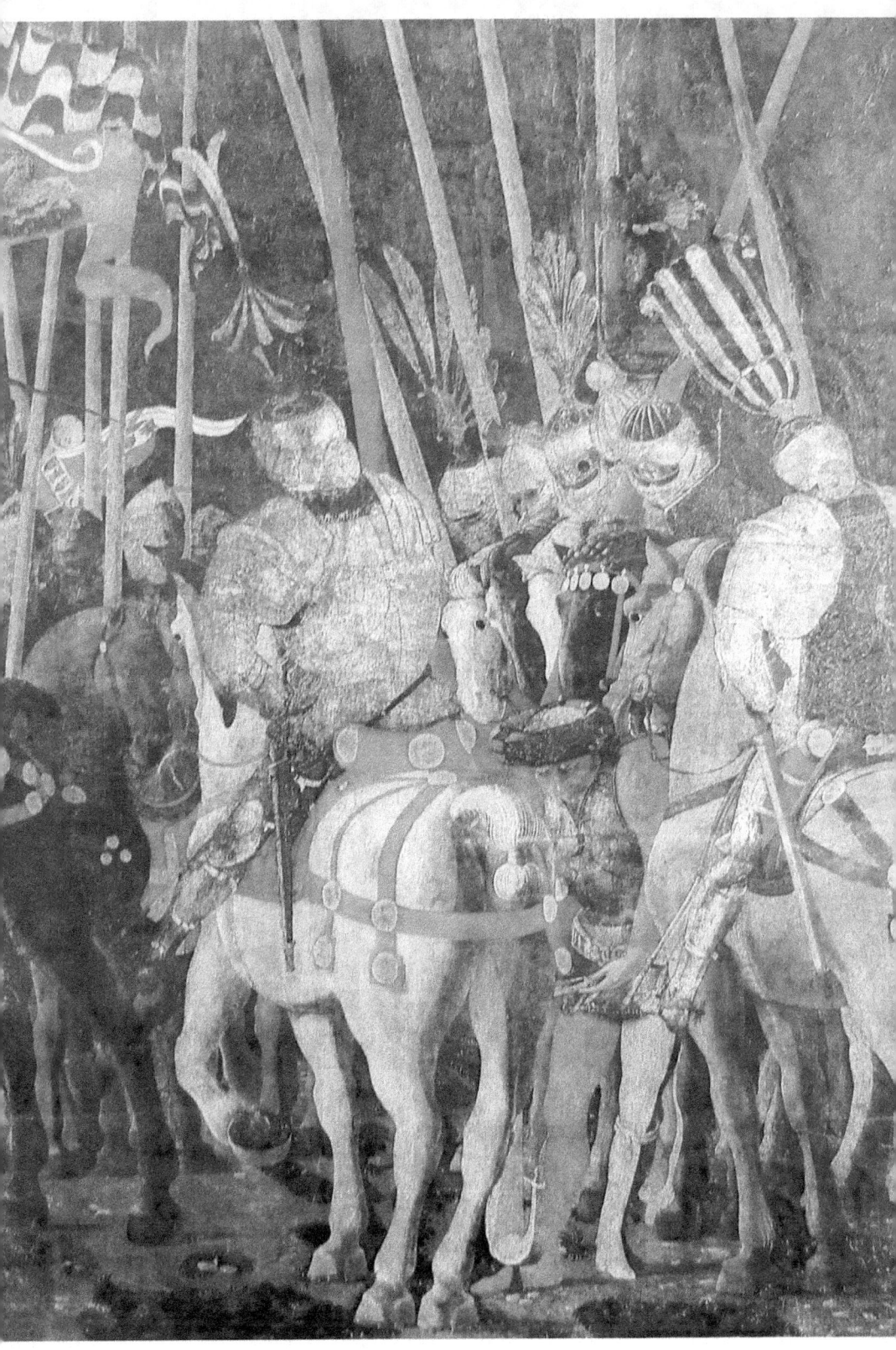

Paolo Uccello, The Battle of San Romano, Paris

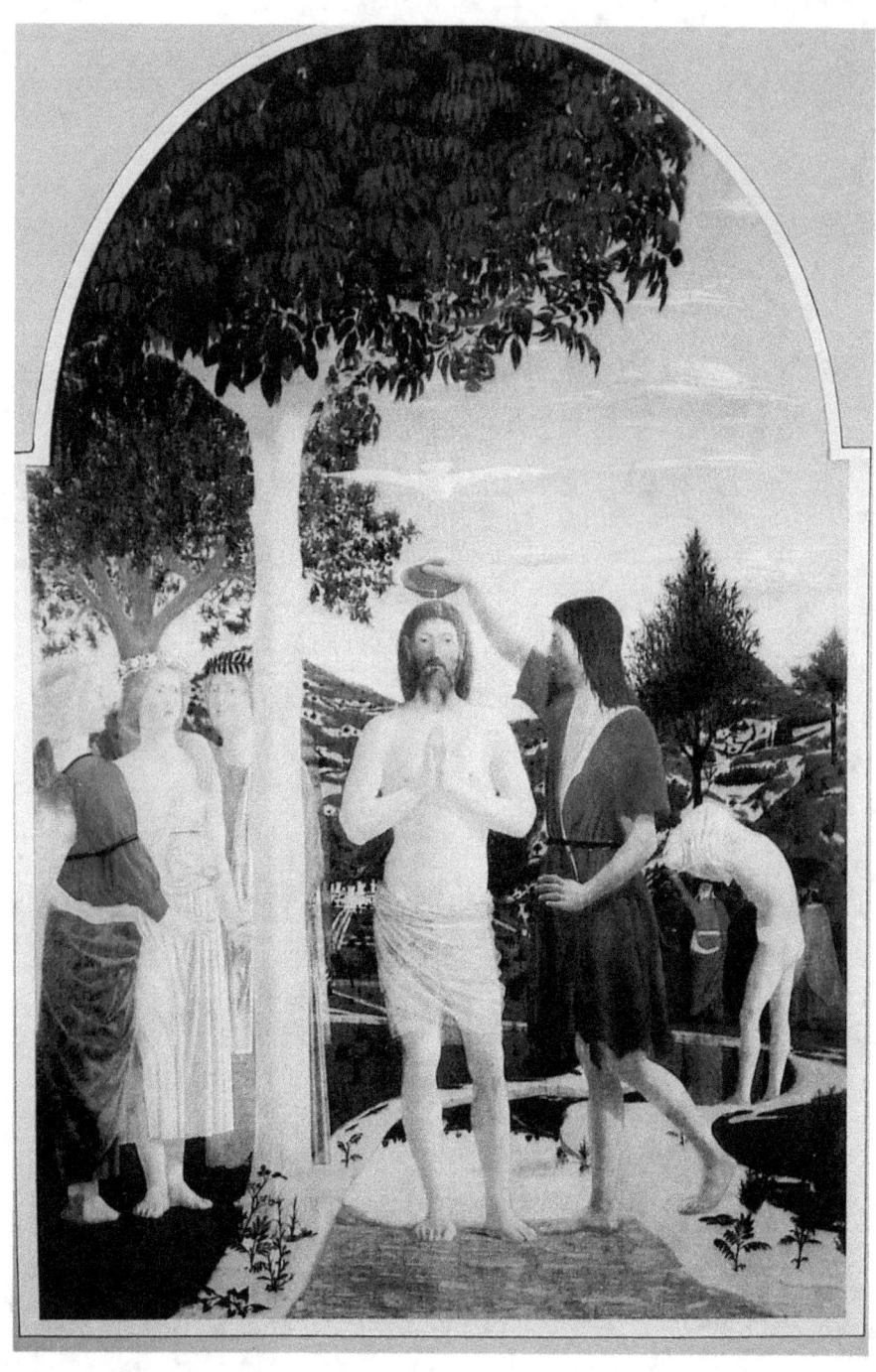

Piero della Francesca, *The Baptism of Christ*, National Gallery,
London

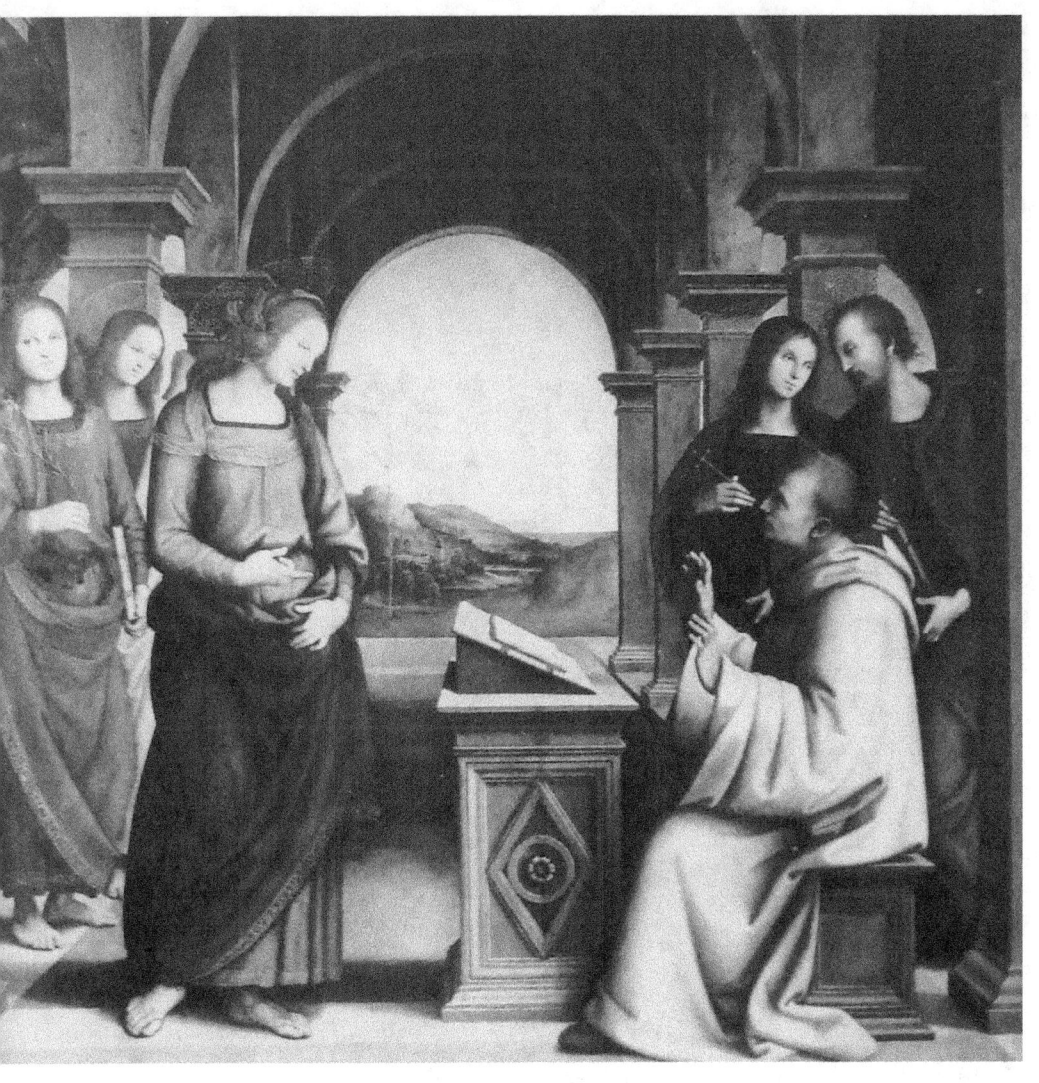

Perugino, Vision of St Bernard, 1488

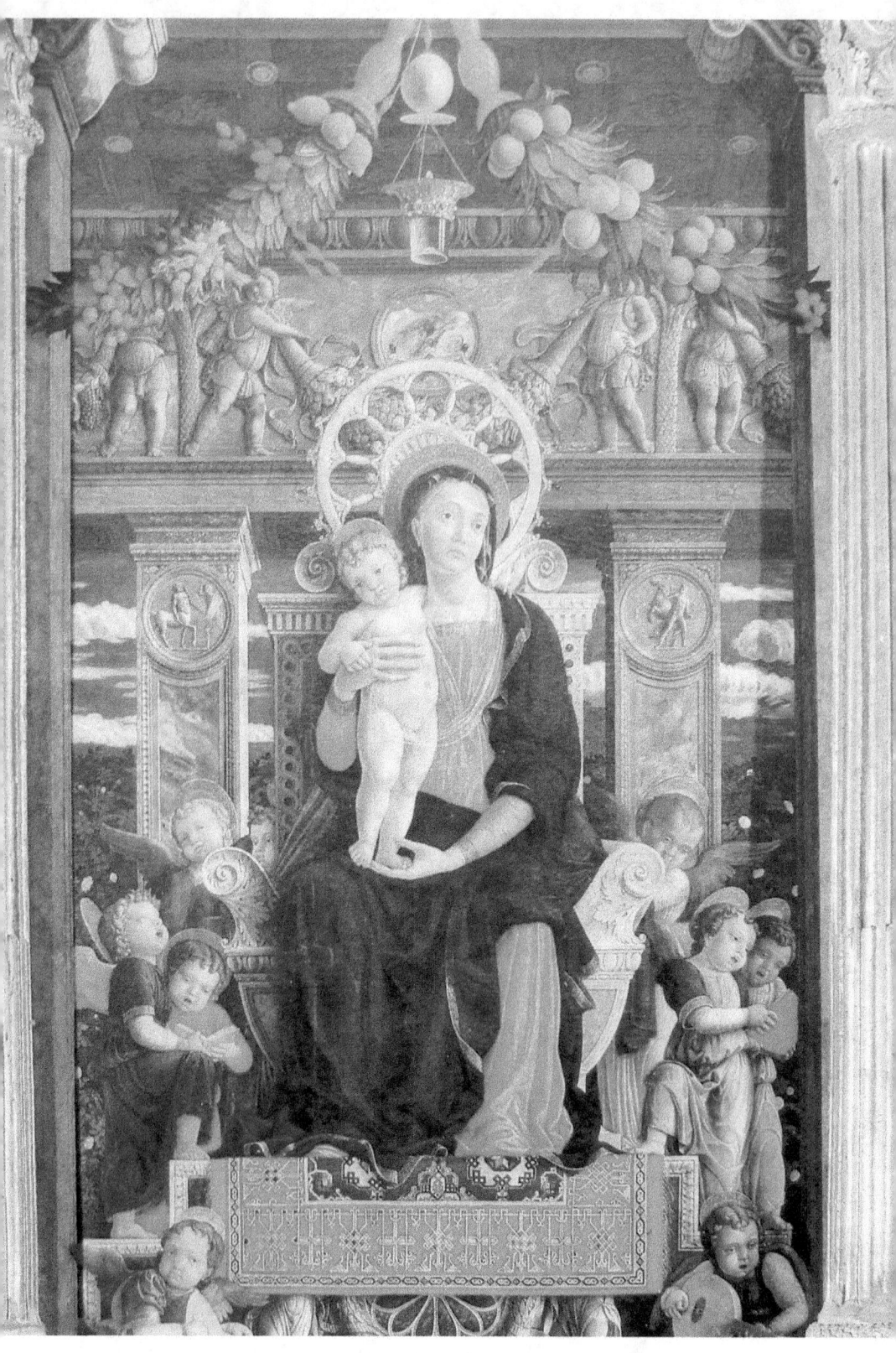

Andreas Mantegna, Madonna and Child Enthroned, 1457-60, Verona

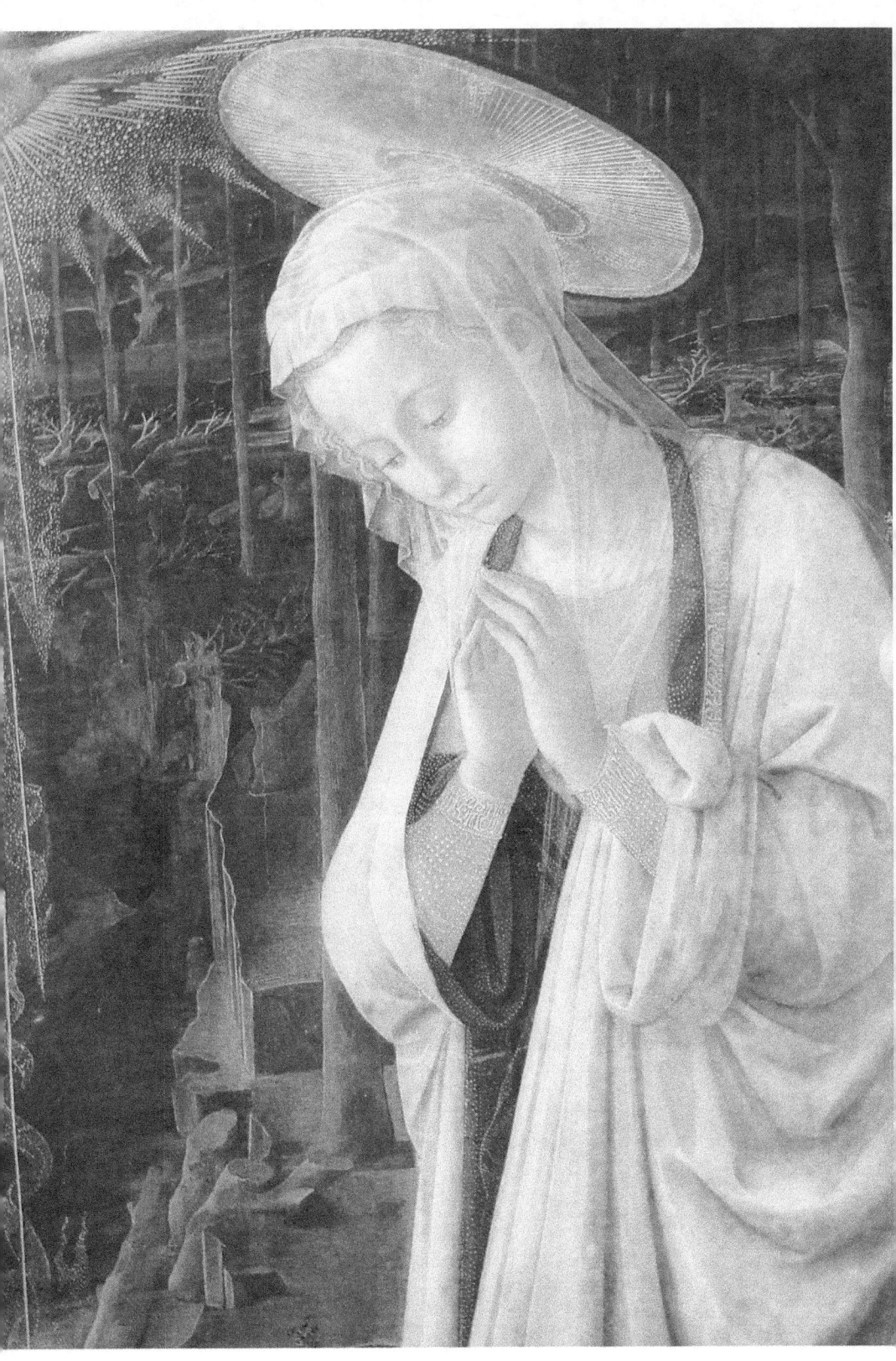

Fra Filippo Lippi, The Adoration of the Virgin, Berlin, detail

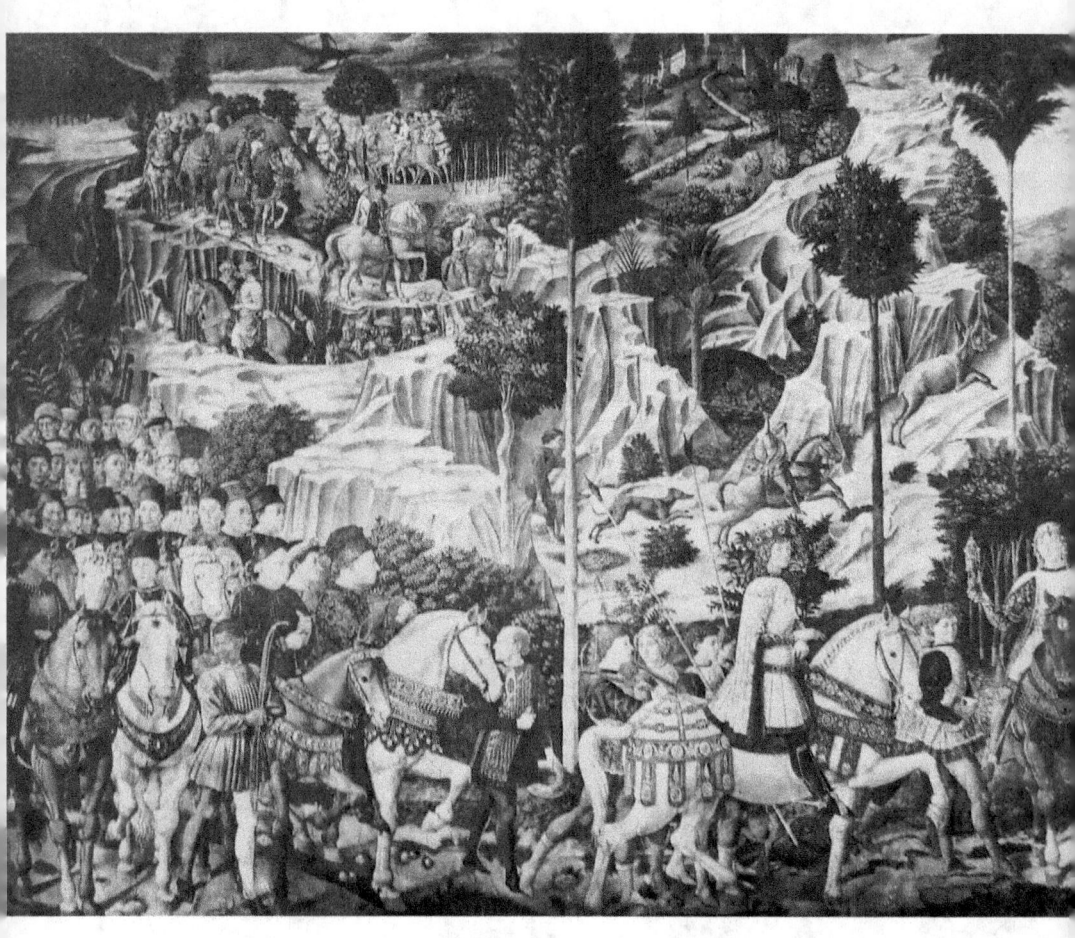

Benozzo Gozzoli, Journey of the Magi

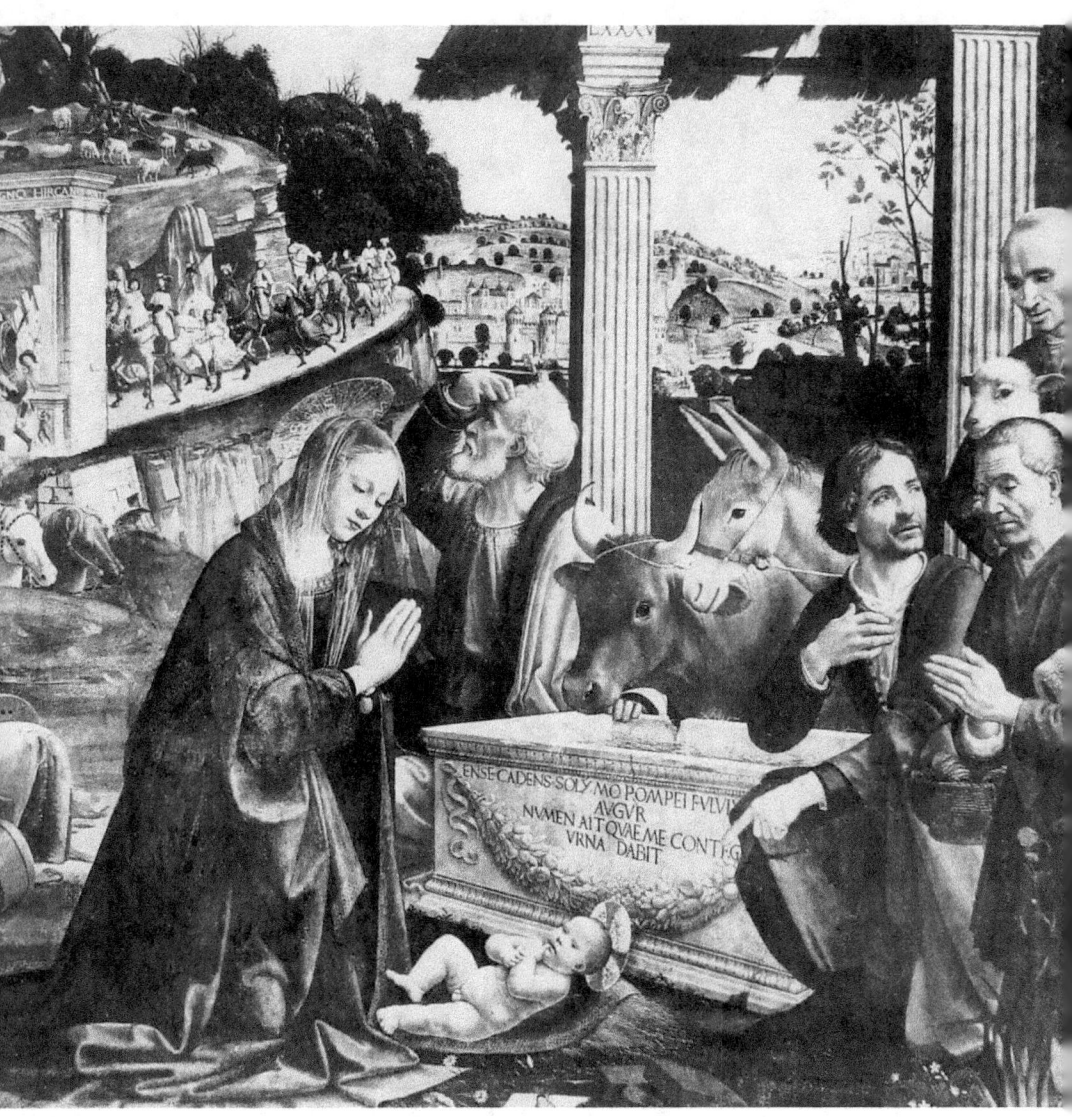

Domenico Ghirlandaio, Adoration of the Shepherds, 1485

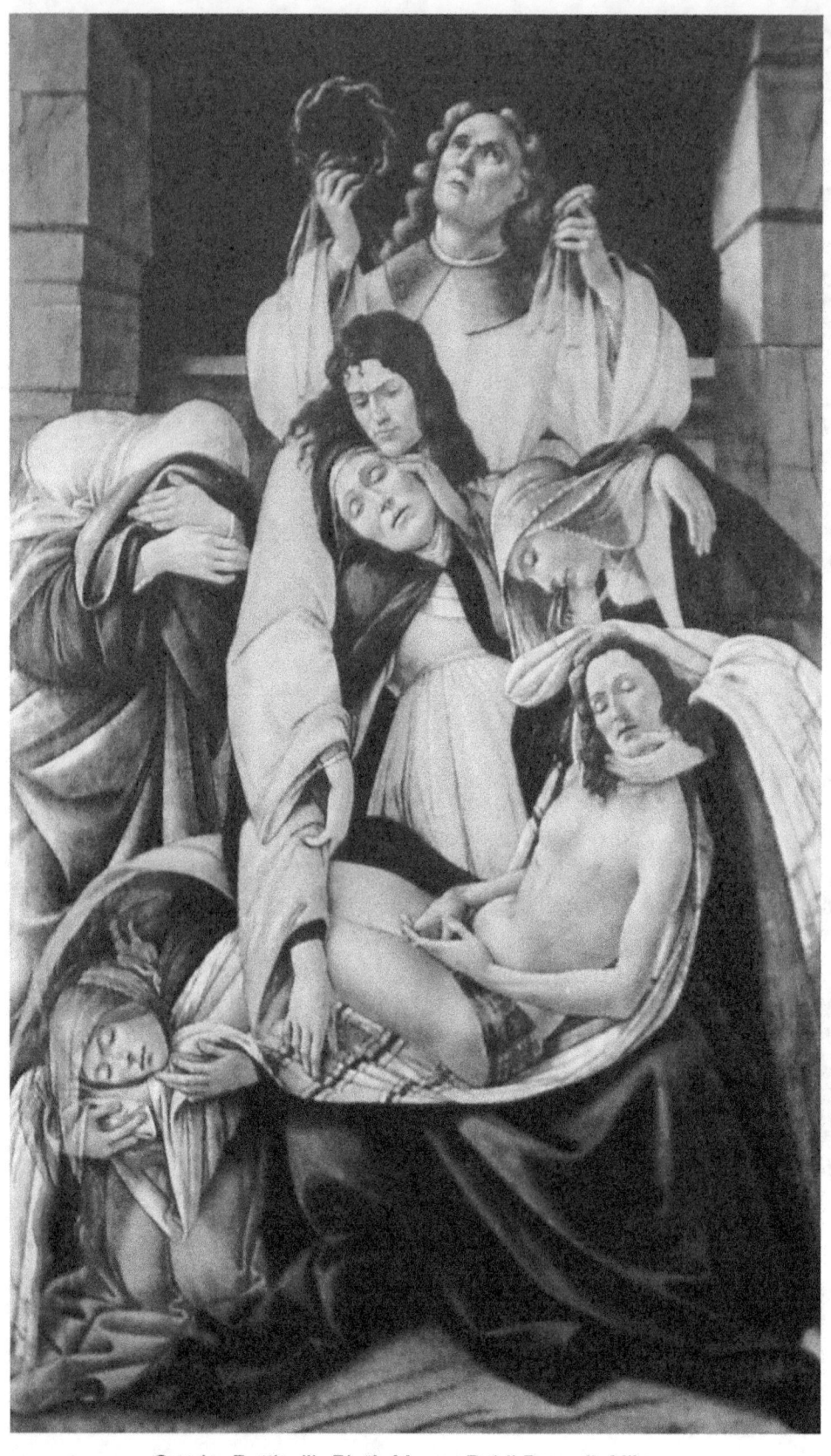

Sandro Botticelli, *Pietà*, Museo Poldi Pezzoli, Milan

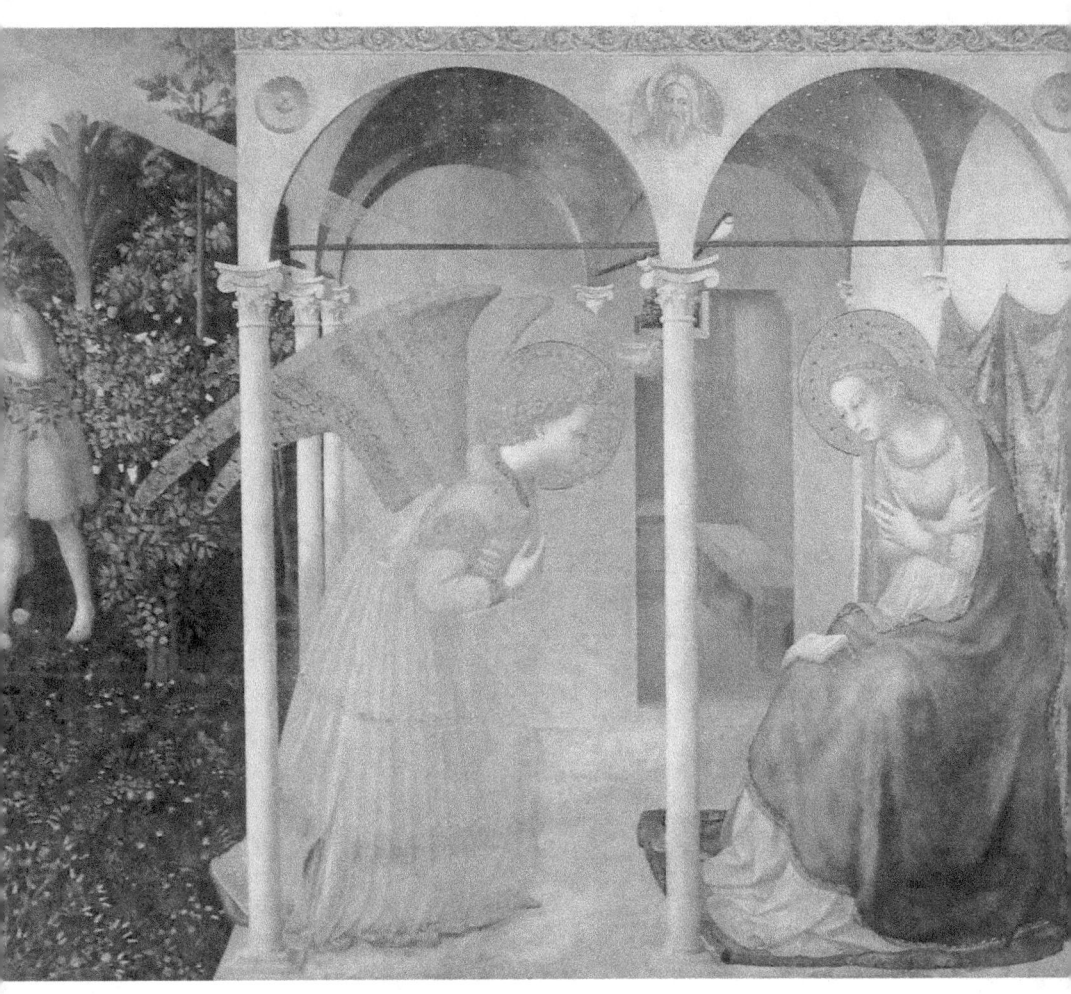

Fra Angelico, Annunciation, Prado, Madrid

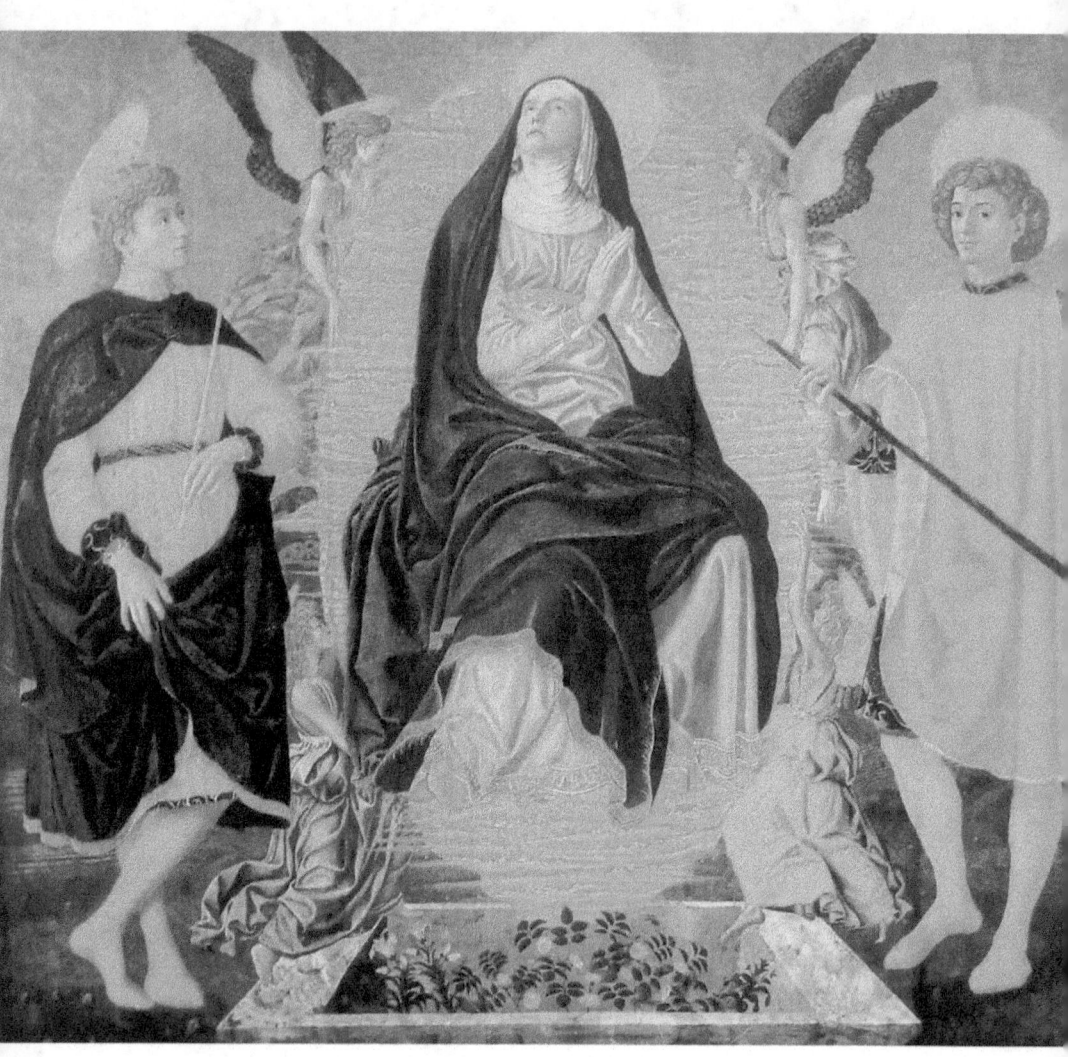

Andrea del Castagno, Assumption, Berlin

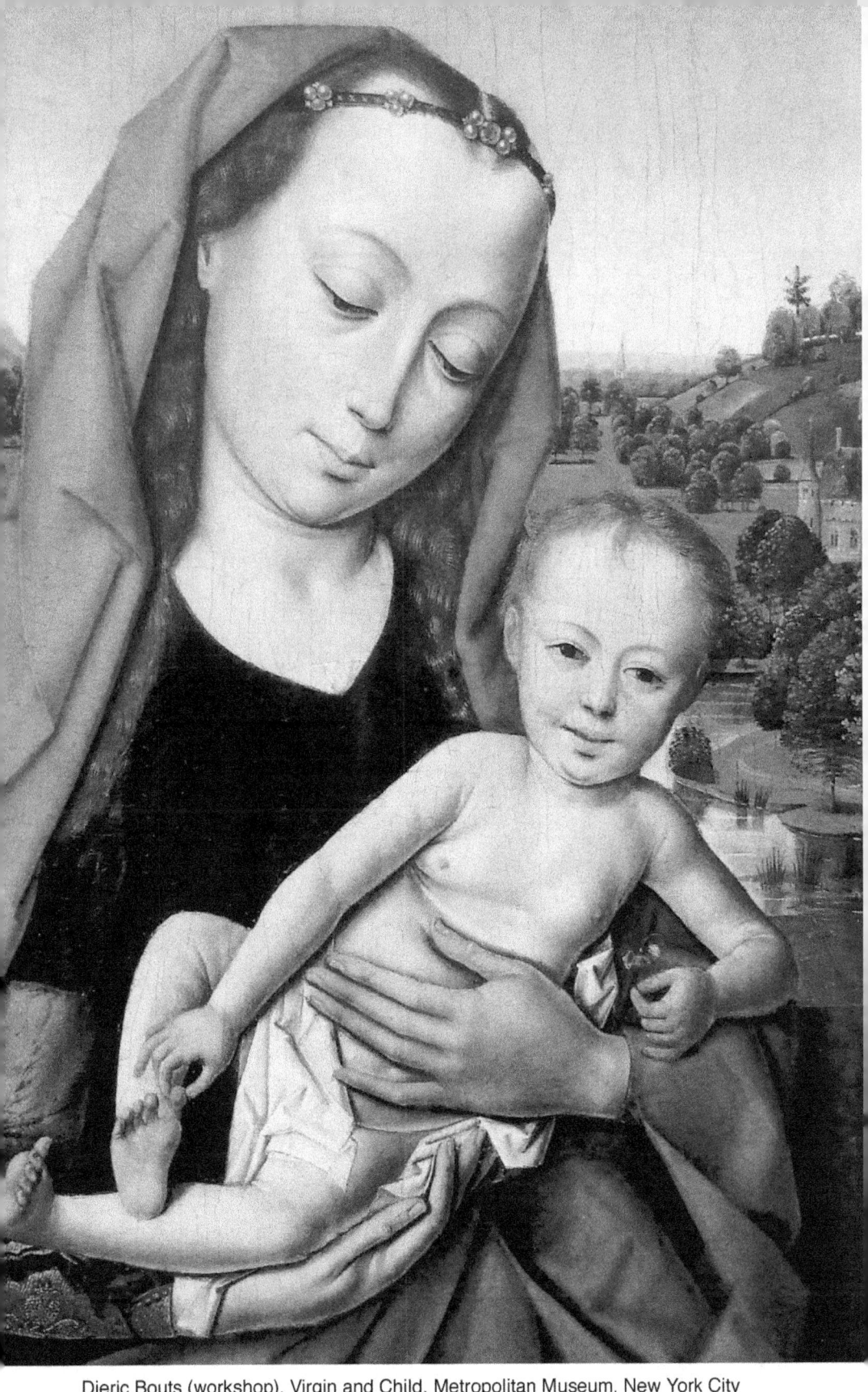

Dieric Bouts (workshop), Virgin and Child, Metropolitan Museum, New York City

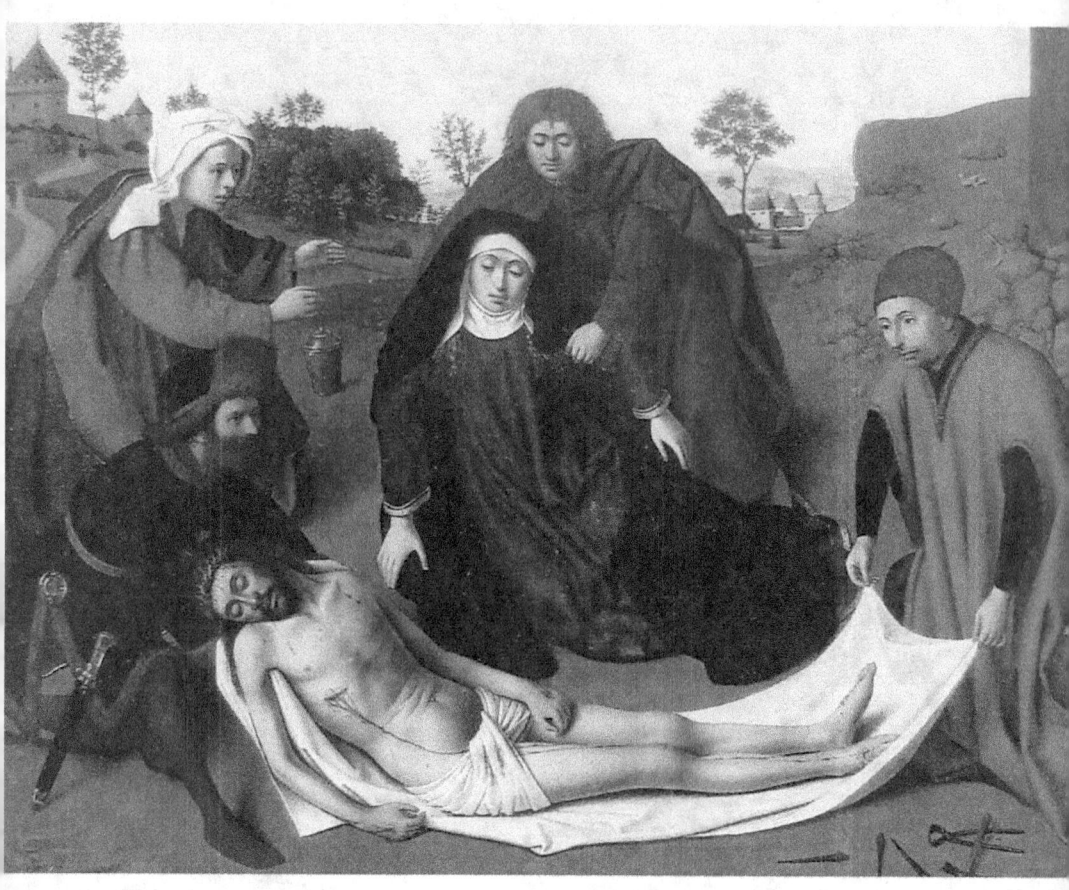

Petrus Christus, The Lamentation, Metropolitan Museum,
New York City

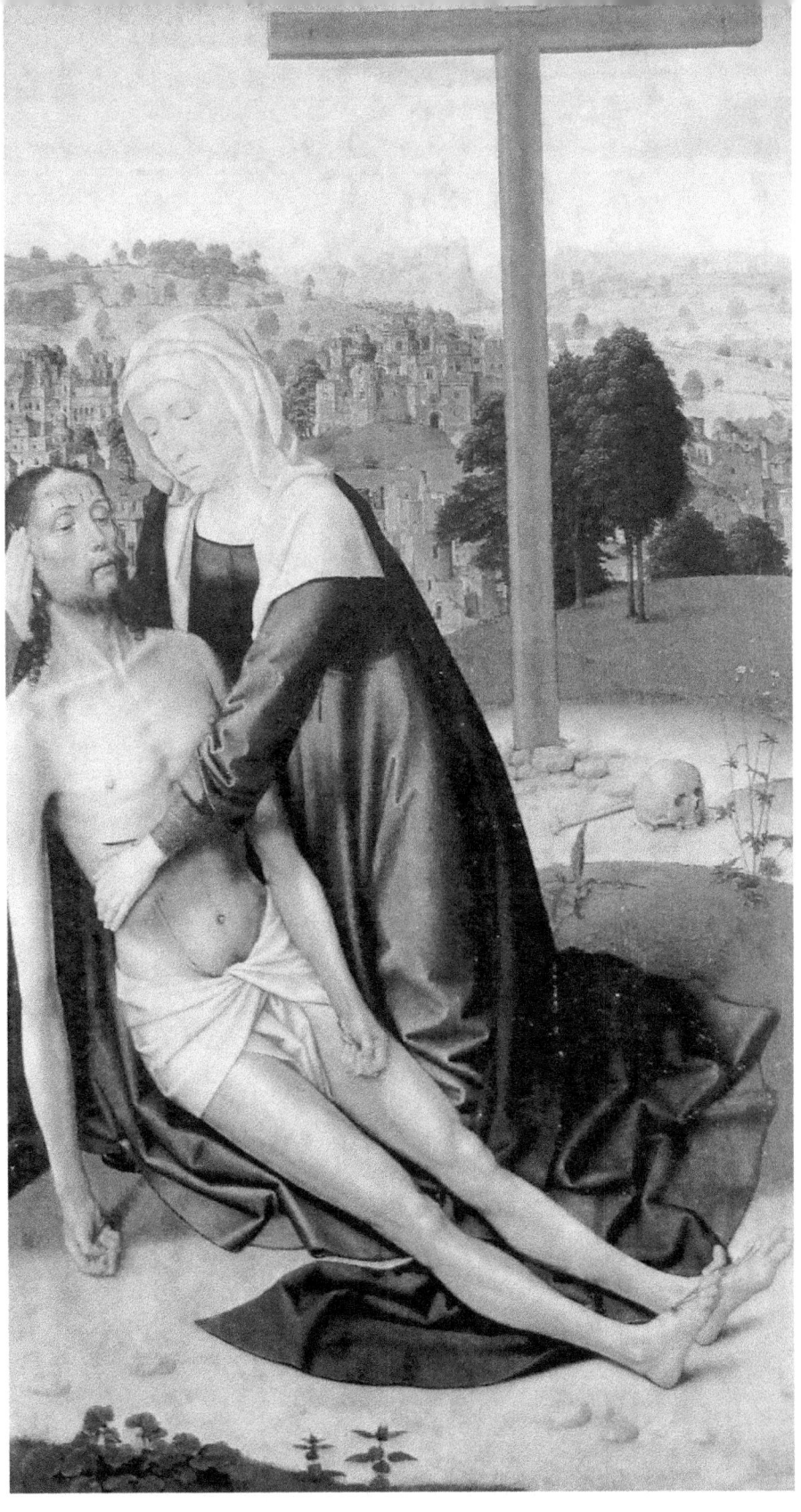

Gerard David, Pietà, Winterhur

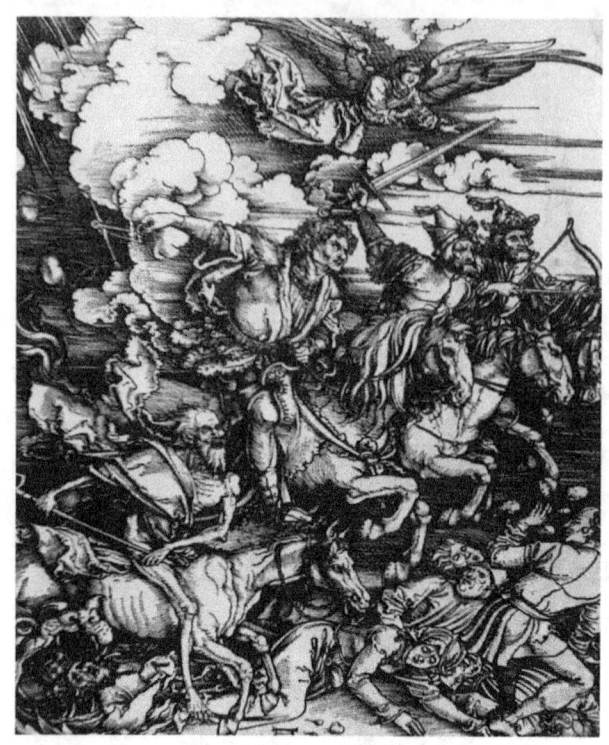

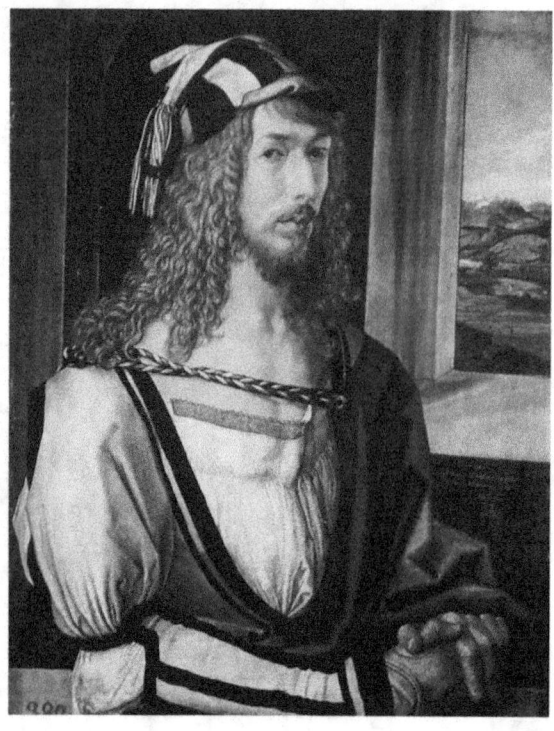

Albrecht Dürer

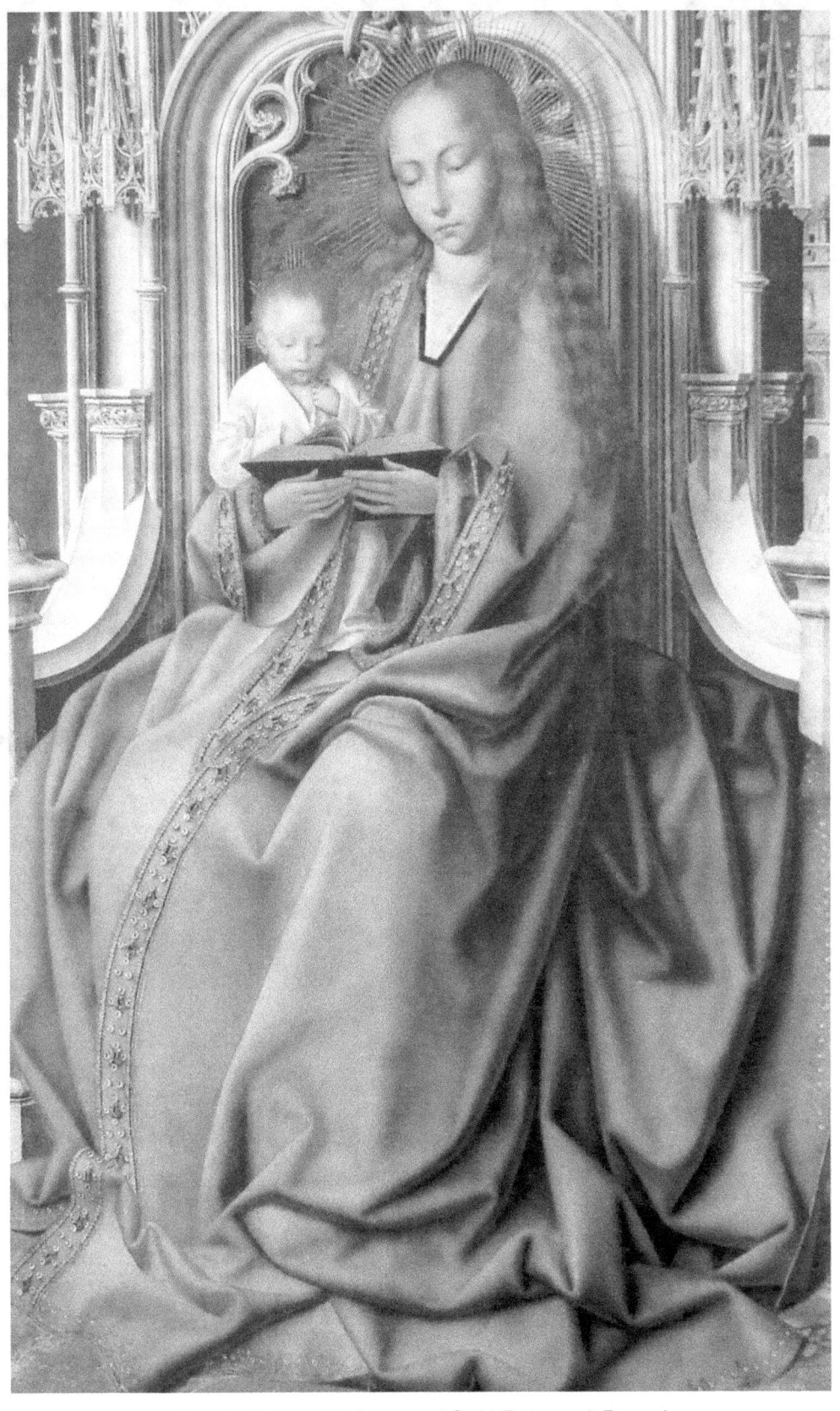

Quentin Massys, Madonna and Child Enthroned, Brussels

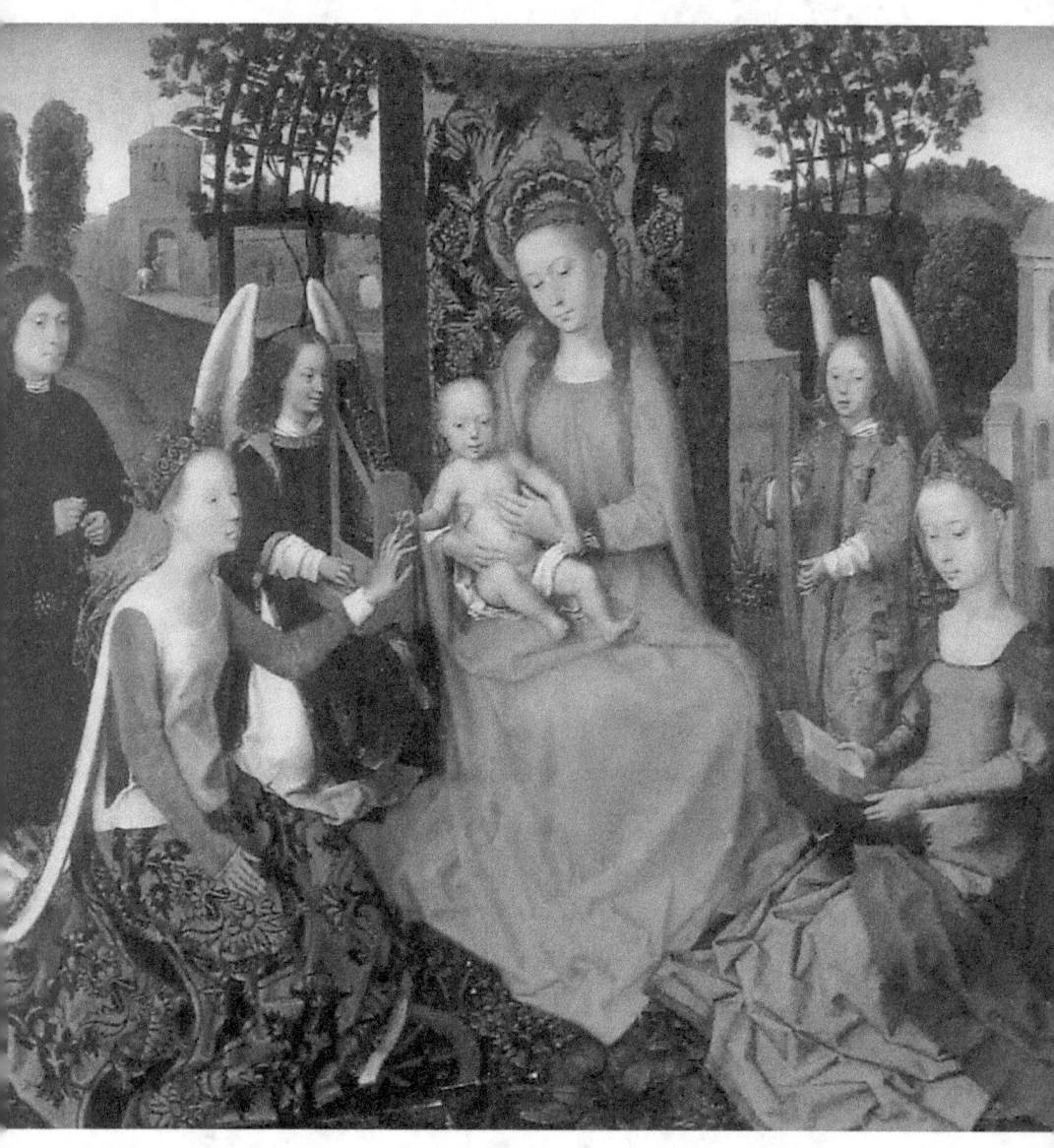

Hans Memling, The Mystic Marriage of St Catherine, Metropolitan
Museum, New York City

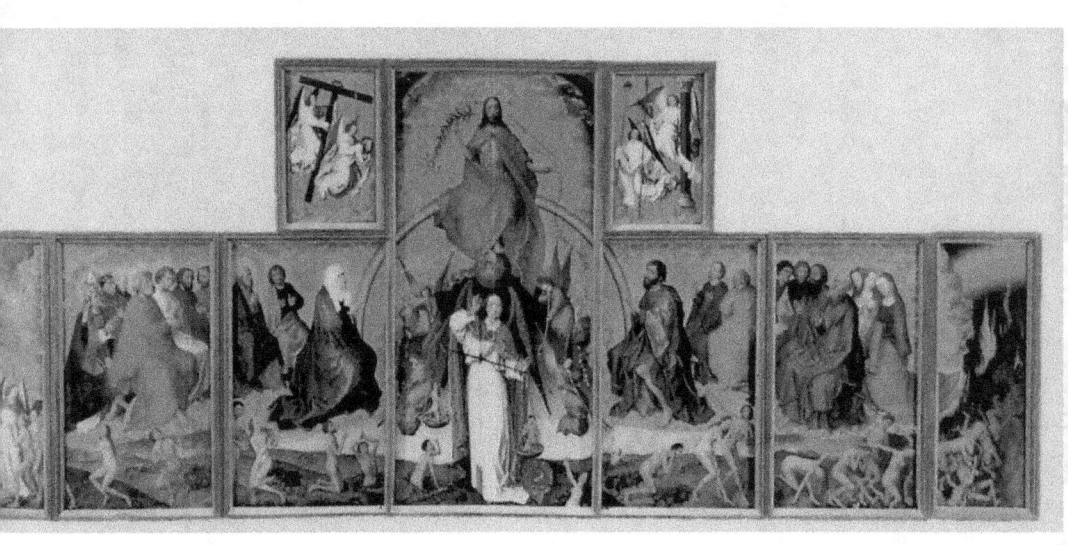

Rogier van der Weyden, The Last Judgement, 1445-49, Beaune

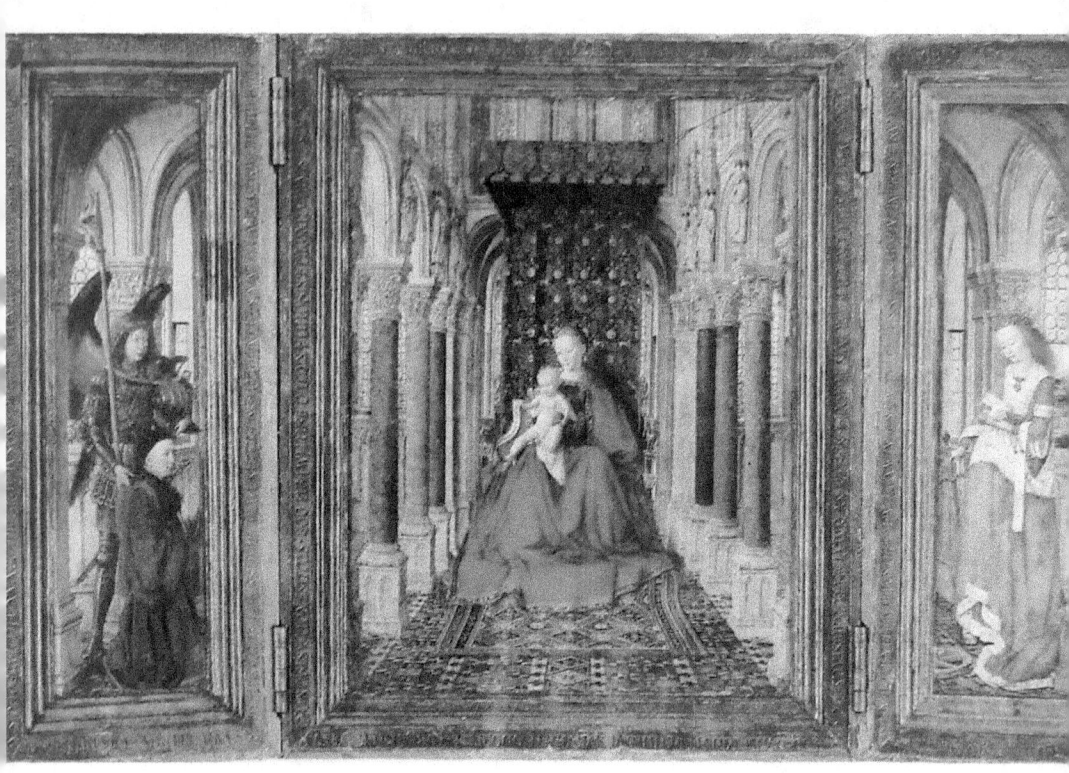

Jan van Eyck, The Dresden Triptych, 1437, Dresden

NOTES ON WORKS

MADONNA AND CHILD.
(In the Wallace Collection)

This is another admirably painted study of the artist's
favourite subject. The attitude of the child is most engaging, the
painting of the limbs is full of skill, and the background adds
considerably to the picture's attractions. It will be noted that Luini
appears to have employed the same model for most of his studies
of the Madonna.

IL SALVATORE
(In the Ambrosiana, Milan)

This picture, one of the treasures of the beautiful collection in
the Pinacoteca of Ambrosiana in the Piazza della Rosa, hangs by
the same artist's picture of "John the Baptist as a Child." The right
hand of Christ is raised in the attitude of benediction, and the
head has a curiously genuine beauty. The preservation of this
picture is wonderful, the colouring retains much of its early glow.
The head is almost feminine in its tenderness and bears a likeness
to Luini's favourite model.

SALOMÉ AND THE HEAD OF ST. JOHN THE BAPTIST
(In the Uffizi Gallery, Florence)

In this striking and finely preserved picture Bernardino Luini has contrived to avoid all sense of horror. The head of the dead John the Baptist is full of beauty, and even Herodias is handled without any attempt to make her repulsive. Sufficient contrast is supplied by the executioner on the right.

THE MYSTIC MARRIAGE OF ST. CATHERINE
(In the Brera, Milan)

This is a singularly attractive picture in which the child Christ may be seen placing the ring upon the finger of St. Catherine. The little open background, although free from the slightest suggestion of Palestine, is very charming, and the head of the Virgin and St. Catherine help to prove that Luini used few models.

THE MADONNA OF THE ROSE
(In the Brera, Milan)

Modern criticism proclaims this picture of the Virgin in a Bower of Roses to be the finest of the master's paintings. Not only is it delightfully composed and thought out but the background is painted with rare skill, and the colour is rich and pleasing to this day.

DETAIL OF FRESCO
(In the Brera, Milan)

This prettily posed figure is at the base of a fresco of the Virgin with Saints in the Brera. Part of the artist's signature (Bernardinus Louinus) may be seen below. It will be remembered that Carpaccio painted a very similar subject. The fresco is not too well preserved.

HEAD OF VIRGIN
(In the Ambrosiana, Milan)

Here we have another well painted and finely preserved head painted from one of Luini's favourite models. The artist must have known most of the secrets of colour preparation, for his work has survived much that was painted centuries later. Unfortunately his frescoes were exposed to the elements and have suffered accordingly.

BURIAL OF ST. CATHERINE
(In the Brera, Milan)

This is one of the frescoes painted by Luini for the Casa Pelucca and transferred to Milan in the beginning of the nineteenth century. It will be seen that although the three angels bearing the Saint to her grave are obviously peasant girls from the plains of Lombardy winged for the occasion, the artist has handled his subject with faith and reverence. The fresco is better preserved than others from the same house.

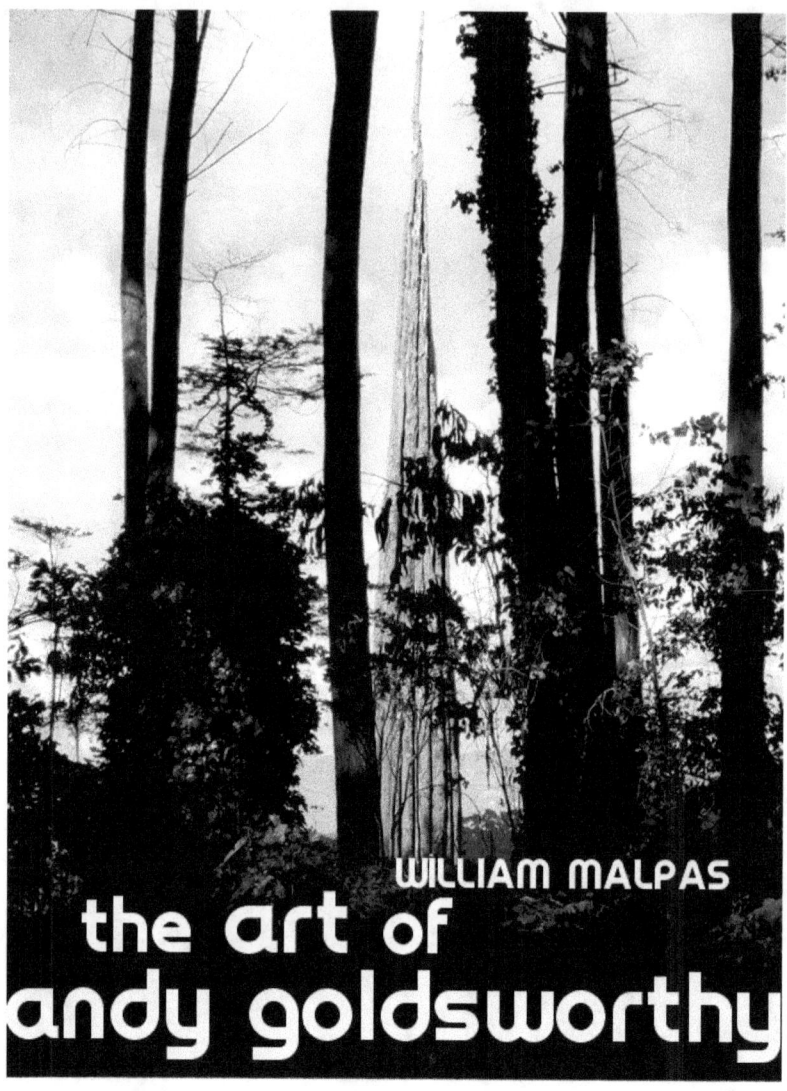

WILLIAM MALPAS
the art of
andy goldsworthy

This is the most comprehensive and detailed account of the art of Andy Goldsworthy available.

This study of Andy Goldsworthy discusses all of Goldsworthy's major exhibitions, books and projects, including the *Sheepfolds* project; *Garden of Stones* in New York; TV and dance collaborations; and the books *Wood, Stone, Time* and *Passage*. William Malpas surveys all of Goldsworthy's output, and analyzes his relation with other land artists such as Robert Smithson, the Christos, Walter de Maria, Chris Drury, Richard Long and David Nash; women sculptors; sculpture in the modern era; and Goldsworthy's place in the contemporary British art scene.

The book has been updated and revised for this new edition.

ISBN 9781861714107 Pbk   ISBN 9781861714114 Hbk
Fully illustrated   www.crmoon.com

MAURICE SENDAK

& the art of children's book illustration

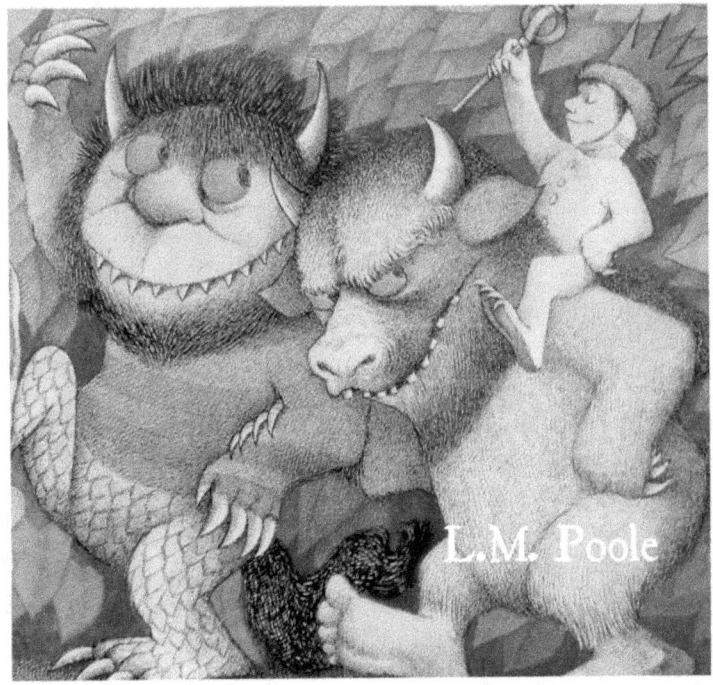

L.M. Poole

Maurice Sendak is the widely acclaimed American children's book author and illustrator. This critical study focuses on his famous trilogy, *Where the Wild Things Are*, *In the Night Kitchen* and *Outside Over There*, as well as the early works and Sendak's superb depictions of the Grimm Brothers' fairy tales in *The Juniper Tree*. L.M. Poole begins with a chapter on children's book illustration, in particular the treatment of fairy tales. Sendak's work is situated within the history of children's book illustration, and he is compared with many contemporary authors.

Fully illustrated. The book has been revised and updated for this edition.

ISBN 9781861714282 Pbk   ISBN 9781861713469 Hbk

Beauties, Beasts, and Enchantment

CLASSIC FRENCH FAIRY TALES

Translated and with an Introduction
by Jack Zipes

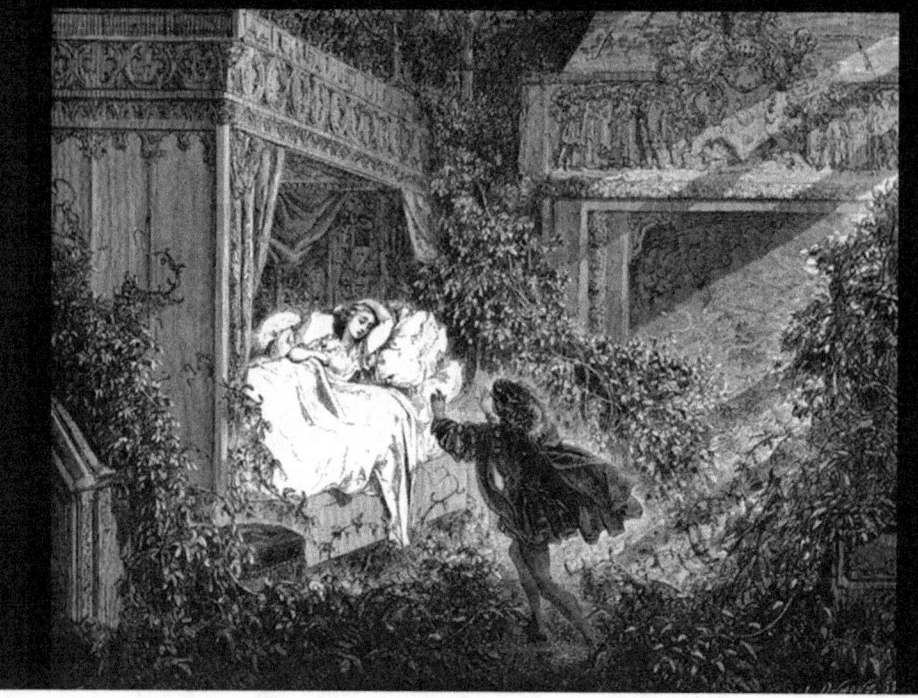

A collection of 36 classic French fairy tales translated by renowned writer Jack Zipes.
Cinderella, Beauty and the Beast, Sleeping Beauty and *Little Red Riding Hood* are among the
classic fairy tales in this amazing book.
Includes illustrations from fairy tale collections.
Jack Zipes has written and published widely on fairy tales.

'Terrific... a succulent array of 17th and 18th century 'salon' fairy tales'
- *The New York Times Book Review*

'These tales are adventurous, thrilling in a way fairy tales are meant to be... The translation
from the French is modern, happily free of archaic and hyperbolic language... a fine and
sophisticated collection' - *New York Tribune*

'Enjoyable to read... a unique collection of French regional folklore' - *Library Journal*

'Charming stories accompanied by attractive pen-and-ink drawings' - *Chattanooga Times*

Introduction and illustrations   612pp.   ISBN 9781861712510 Pbk   ISBN 9781861713193 Hbk

CRESCENT MOON PUBLISHING

web: www.crmoon.com e-mail: cresmopub@yahoo.co.uk

ARTS, PAINTING, SCULPTURE

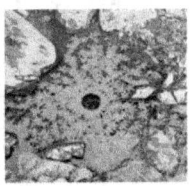

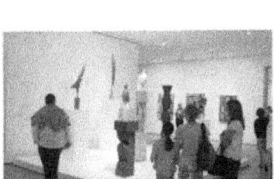

The Art of Andy Goldsworthy
Andy Goldsworthy: Touching Nature
Andy Goldsworthy in Close-Up
Andy Goldsworthy: Pocket Guide
Andy Goldsworthy In America
Land Art: A Complete Guide
The Art of Richard Long
Richard Long: Pocket Guide
Land Art In the UK
Land Art in Close-Up
Land Art In the U.S.A.
Land Art: Pocket Guide
Installation Art in Close-Up
Minimal Art and Artists In the 1960s and After
Colourfield Painting
Land Art DVD, TV documentary
Andy Goldsworthy DVD, TV documentary
The Erotic Object: Sexuality in Sculpture From Prehistory to the Present Day
Sex in Art: Pornography and Pleasure in Painting and Sculpture
Postwar Art
Sacred Gardens: The Garden in Myth, Religion and Art
Glorification: Religious Abstraction in Renaissance and 20th Century Art
Early Netherlandish Painting
Leonardo da Vinci
Piero della Francesca
Giovanni Bellini
Fra Angelico: Art and Religion in the Renaissance
Mark Rothko: The Art of Transcendence
Frank Stella: American Abstract Artist
Jasper Johns
Brice Marden
Alison Wilding: The Embrace of Sculpture
Vincent van Gogh: Visionary Landscapes
Eric Gill: Nuptials of God
Constantin Brancusi: Sculpting the Essence of Things
Max Beckmann
Caravaggio
Gustave Moreau
Egon Schiele: Sex and Death In Purple Stockings
Delizioso Fotografico Fervore: Works In Process 1
Sacro Cuore: Works In Process 2
The Light Eternal: J.M.W. Turner
The Madonna Glorified: Karen Arthurs

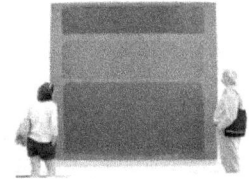

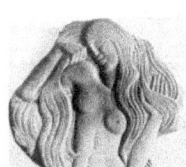

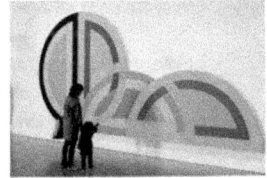

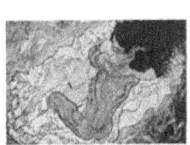

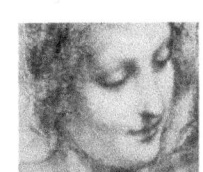

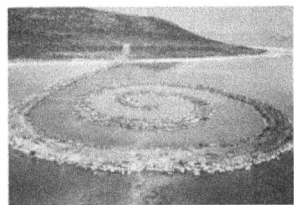

LITERATURE

J.R.R. Tolkien: The Books, The Films, The Whole Cultural Phenomenon
J.R.R. Tolkien: Pocket Guide
Tolkien's Heroic Quest
The *Earthsea* Books of Ursula Le Guin
Beauties, Beasts and Enchantment: Classic French Fairy Tales
German Popular Stories by the Brothers Grimm
Philip Pullman and *His Dark Materials*
Sexing Hardy: Thomas Hardy and Feminism
Thomas Hardy's *Tess of the d'Urbervilles*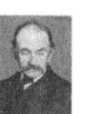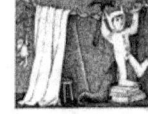
Thomas Hardy's *Jude the Obscure*
Thomas Hardy: The Tragic Novels
Love and Tragedy: Thomas Hardy
The Poetry of Landscape in Hardy
Wessex Revisited: Thomas Hardy and John Cowper Powys
Wolfgang Iser: Essays and Interviews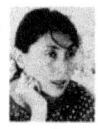
Petrarch, Dante and the Troubadours
Maurice Sendak and the Art of Children's Book Illustration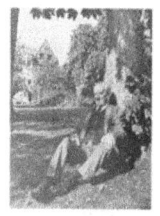
Andrea Dworkin
Cixous, Irigaray, Kristeva: The *Jouissance* of French Feminism
Julia Kristeva: Art, Love, Melancholy, Philosophy, Semiotics and Psychoanalysis
Hélene Cixous I Love You: The *Jouissance* of Writing
Luce Irigaray: Lips, Kissing, and the Politics of Sexual Difference
Peter Redgrove: Here Comes the Flood
Peter Redgrove: Sex-Magic-Poetry-Cornwall
Lawrence Durrell: Between Love and Death, East and West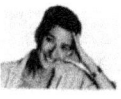
Love, Culture & Poetry: Lawrence Durrell
Cavafy: Anatomy of a Soul
German Romantic Poetry: Goethe, Novalis, Heine, Hölderlin
Feminism and Shakespeare
Shakespeare: Love, Poetry & Magic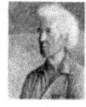
The Passion of D.H. Lawrence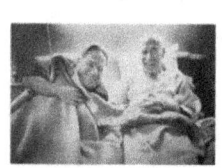
D.H. Lawrence: Symbolic Landscapes
D.H. Lawrence: Infinite Sensual Violence
Rimbaud: Arthur Rimbaud and the Magic of Poetry
The Ecstasies of John Cowper Powys
Sensualism and Mythology: The Wessex Novels of John Cowper Powys
Amorous Life: John Cowper Powys and the Manifestation of Affectivity (H.W. Fawkner)
Postmodern Powys: New Essays on John Cowper Powys (Joe Boulter)
Rethinking Powys: Critical Essays on John Cowper Powys
Paul Bowles & Bernardo Bertolucci
Rainer Maria Rilke
Joseph Conrad: *Heart of Darkness*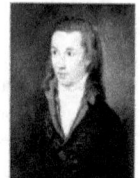
In the Dim Void: Samuel Beckett
Samuel Beckett Goes into the Silence
André Gide: Fiction and Fervour
Jackie Collins and the Blockbuster Novel
Blinded By Her Light: The Love-Poetry of Robert Graves
The Passion of Colours: Travels In Mediterranean Lands
Poetic Forms

POETRY

Ursula Le Guin: Walking In Cornwall
Peter Redgrove: Here Comes The Flood
Peter Redgrove: Sex-Magic-Poetry-Cornwall
Dante: Selections From the Vita Nuova
Petrarch, Dante and the Troubadours
William Shakespeare: Sonnets
William Shakespeare: Complete Poems
Blinded By Her Light: The Love-Poetry of Robert Graves
Emily Dickinson: Selected Poems
Emily Brontë: Poems
Thomas Hardy: Selected Poems
Percy Bysshe Shelley: Poems
John Keats: Selected Poems
Joh n Keats: Poems of 1820
D.H. Lawrence: Selected Poems
Edmund Spenser: Poems
Edmund Spenser: Amoretti
John Donne: Poems
Henry Vaughan: Poems
Sir Thomas Wyatt: Poems
Robert Herrick: Selected Poems
Rilke: Space, Essence and Angels in the Poetry of Rainer Maria Rilke
Rainer Maria Rilke: Selected Poems
Friedrich Hölderlin: Selected Poems
Arseny Tarkovsky: Selected Poems
Arthur Rimbaud: Selected Poems
Arthur Rimbaud: A Season in Hell
Arthur Rimbaud and the Magic of Poetry
Novalis: Hymns To the Night
German Romantic Poetry
Paul Verlaine: Selected Poems
Elizaethan Sonnet Cycles
D.J. Enright: By-Blows
Jeremy Reed: Brigitte's Blue Heart
Jeremy Reed: Claudia Schiffer's Red Shoes
Gorgeous Little Orpheus
Radiance: New Poems
Crescent Moon Book of Nature Poetry
Crescent Moon Book of Love Poetry
Crescent Moon Book of Mystical Poetry
Crescent Moon Book of Elizabethan Love Poetry
Crescent Moon Book of Metaphysical Poetry
Crescent Moon Book of Romantic Poetry
Pagan America: New American Poetry

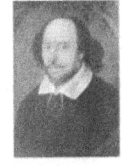
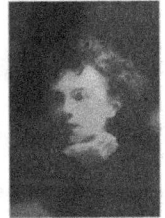
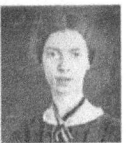
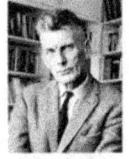
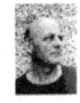
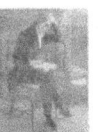
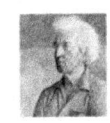
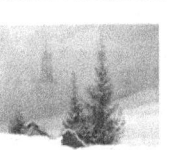
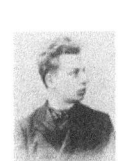
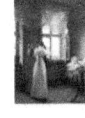
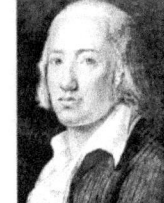
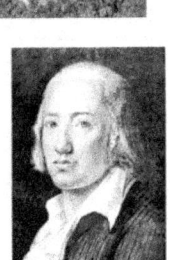

MEDIA, CINEMA, FEMINISM and CULTURAL STUDIES

J.R.R. Tolkien: The Books, The Films, The Whole Cultural Phenomenon
J.R.R. Tolkien: Pocket Guide
The *Lord of the Rings* Movies: Pocket Guide
The Cinema of Hayao Miyazaki
Hayao Miyazaki: *Princess Mononoke*: Pocket Movie Guide
Hayao Miyazaki: *Spirited Away*: Pocket Movie Guide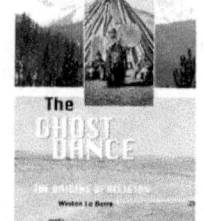
Tim Burton : Hallowe'en For Hollywood
Ken Russell
Ken Russell: *Tommy*: Pocket Movie Guide
The Ghost Dance: The Origins of Religion
The Peyote Cult
Cixous, Irigaray, Kristeva: The *Jouissance* of French Feminism
Julia Kristeva: Art, Love, Melancholy, Philosophy, Semiotics and Psychoanalysis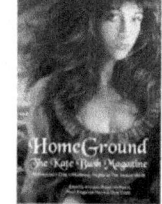
Luce Irigaray: Lips, Kissing, and the Politics of Sexual Difference
Hélène Cixous I Love You: The *Jouissance* of Writing
Andrea Dworkin
'Cosmo Woman': The World of Women's Magazines
Women in Pop Music
HomeGround: The Kate Bush Anthology
Discovering the Goddess (Geoffrey Ashe)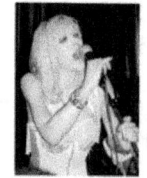
The Poetry of Cinema
The Sacred Cinema of Andrei Tarkovsky
Andrei Tarkovsky: Pocket Guide
Andrei Tarkovsky: *Mirror*: Pocket Movie Guide
Andrei Tarkovsky: *The Sacrifice*: Pocket Movie Guide
Walerian Borowczyk: Cinema of Erotic Dreams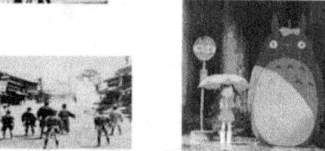
Jean-Luc Godard: The Passion of Cinema
Jean-Luc Godard: *Hail Mary*: Pocket Movie Guide
Jean-Luc Godard: *Contempt*: Pocket Movie Guide
Jean-Luc Godard: *Pierrot le Fou*: Pocket Movie Guide
John Hughes and Eighties Cinema
Ferris Bueller's Day Off: Pocket Movie Guide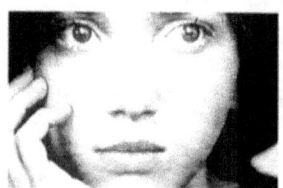
Jean-Luc Godard: Pocket Guide
The Cinema of Richard Linklater
Liv Tyler: Star In Ascendance
Blade Runner and the Films of Philip K. Dick
Paul Bowles and Bernardo Bertolucci
Media Hell: Radio, TV and the Press
An Open Letter to the BBC
Detonation Britain: Nuclear War in the UK
Feminism and Shakespeare
Wild Zones: Pornography, Art and Feminism
Sex in Art: Pornography and Pleasure in Painting and Sculpture
Sexing Hardy: Thomas Hardy and Feminism

The Light Eternal is a model monograph, an exemplary job. The subject matter of the book is beautifully organised and dead on beam. (Lawrence Durrell)
It is amazing for me to see my work treated with such passion and respect. (Andrea Dworkin)

CRESCENT MOON PUBLISHING
P.O. Box 1312, Maidstone, Kent, ME14 5XU, Great Britain. www.crmoon.com

cresmopub@yahoo.co.uk   www.crescentmoon.org.uk